PEACE THINKING
IN A
WARRING WORLD

Books by Edward LeRoy Long, Jr.
Published by The Westminster Press

Peace Thinking in a Warring World
War and Conscience in America
The Role of the Self in Conflicts and Struggle
*Conscience and Compromise: An Outline of Protestant
    Casuistry*
Religious Beliefs of American Scientists
The Christian Response to the Atomic Crisis

Edited by Edward LeRoy Long, Jr., and Robert T. Handy

Theology and Church in Times of Change

PEACE THINKING
IN A
WARRING WORLD

by
Edward LeRoy Long, Jr.

The Westminster Press
Philadelphia

Copyright © 1983 Edward LeRoy Long, Jr.

Scripture quotations from the Revised Standard Version of the Bible are copyrighted 1946, 1952, © 1971, 1973 by the Division of Christian Education of the National Council of the Churches of Christ in the U.S.A., and are used by permission.

BOOK DESIGN BY ALICE DERR

First edition

Published by The Westminster Press ®
Philadelphia, Pennsylvania

PRINTED IN THE UNITED STATES OF AMERICA
9 8 7 6 5 4 3 2 1

Library of Congress Cataloging in Publication Data

Long, Edward Le Roy.
    Peace thinking in a warring world.

    Includes bibliographical references.
    1. Peace (Theology)   2. War—Religious aspects—
Christianity.   I. Title.
BT736.4.L66 1983   261.8′73   83-14675
ISBN 0-664-24503-X (pbk.)

To
PAUL L. MEACHAM

For many years a skilled editor
and cherished friend

*Who at the very beginning of my career
saw possibilities in my writing,
and who very near to his retirement
did much for this volume*

Contents

Foreword

For too long we have thought about war and peace in terms of handling war as a problem rather than seeking peace as an achievement. Today we are engaged in a massive arms race with weaponry of unprecedented and almost inconceivably destructive power. We are making national policy with a mind-set dominated almost entirely by military solutions to international issues. The present situation, with all its potential for destroying much of known civilization and even perhaps ending the future prospects of the race, does not intrude into our consciousness as starkly as did the scenes of slaughter and horror that television screens carried during the Vietnam conflict. It must be sensed more abstractly and intellectually. But the reality of the problem is just as great, and the stakes are much higher. Is there no way to face the future other than to build more and bigger instruments of destruction and pray that they will never be used?

We need to discover what it means to make peace rather than how to respond conscientiously to the problem of war. We must learn to think and to act in ways that will, we hope, head off a widespread and world-destroying conflict. What is said in this volume is of necessity more tentative and exploratory than what it is possible to say about war as a problem for conscience. Christian teaching about the morality of participating in war, despite the fact that it never reached agreement, emerged as three positions with a long gestation and well-expressed arguments. For some time it has been possible to distill them and to be confident of correctly representing the different points of view. In contrast, Christian thinking about peacemaking and overcoming the conditions that make for war is still feeling its way along. We all have to start almost anew to learn how to think about the things that make for peace. If what follows helps in even a small way to advance this discussion, the risks and ventures in thinking beyond the orbit of acknowledged formulations will be worthwhile.

Because this book has been prepared for a general readership, it does not laboriously discuss all the issues that would concern the highly trained theologian. I have, nevertheless, kept in mind contemporary theological interests, and I thread a middle way between the point of view known for some four decades as Christian realism and one known for a little over a decade as liberation theology. Christian realism is now claimed as a heritage by theologians and political philosophers who come to surprisingly divergent judgments about the issues of war and peace in a nuclear age. Some of them place a greater reliance upon the harsh use of power than is compatible with the original intentions of Christian realists. I disassociate myself from that reductionism. Liberation theologies offer a contrast to realism. They are frequently so concerned with freedom, and so concerned to challenge the repressive use of power, that they do not always give sufficient attention to the necessity of order or of compassion in political affairs. Here I gently nudge them to do so. Throughout the treatment that follows, considerable attention is devoted to showing that relationships between persons in small and intimate contexts and in large and impersonal ones must be subjected to the same moral expectations. This is a break with thinking that has treated these two levels as sharply different. About these matters the highly professional reader will have to wait for the development elsewhere of the theoretical scaffolding that would support the argument of this book.

Any work such as this stems from many experiences. Toward the end of the Vietnam War, I explored in *War and Conscience in America* the changing nature of war and considered the responses that Christians might make in good faith to the moral dilemmas posed by a small, brutal, and apparently unproductive military engagement on the far side of an ocean. I have received numerous requests to update or reprint that work, but I have written this book instead to indicate the lines along which I now feel our thinking must go in response to an even more threatening set of developments. My interest in these matters was propelled forward by working on the United Presbyterian task force that produced a study called *Peacemaking: The Believers' Calling.* Subsequently I have taught courses about these issues at Drew Theological School, at Princeton Theological Seminary, and at the Institute of Theology of the Cathedral Church of St. John the Divine. This book contains thinking about these matters more concise and yet more fully developed than that given in those courses and lectures.

In writing this book I have learned that I live in peace with many friends. Dr. Charles Courtney of Drew University, Dr. Robert Smylie of the United Presbyterian Program Agency, and Dr. Alan Geyer of The Churches' Center for Theology and Public Policy have each read a preliminary draft and offered suggestions that did much to make possible the rather complete recasting that is finalized here. I am profoundly grateful to them. Dr. Paul L. Meacham of The Westminster Press and my wife, Grace, rode hard on my verbiage so that such clarity as has emerged is largely due to their efforts on the reader's behalf.

All of us are only beginning to think hard enough about the issues addressed in this book. We see them as yet only dimly, but we do perceive the need for light. Perhaps years of work will be required to replace war-oriented thinking with peace-oriented thinking. Let the reader join in the prayer that we shall be given those years in which to render our service to God by thinking and acting for peace in this warring world.

E.L.L. Jr.

Drew Forest
Madison, New Jersey

I

From War Thinking to Peace Thinking

Almost everyone yearns to live in peace. There may be a few exceptions, such as opportunists who earn fortunes selling arms and mercenaries who seek adventure using them. A small minority that extols conflict as a means of building toughness and of proving national mettle may disagree. But most of us believe that the nations of the world were intended to live peacefully with one another and not to be continually engaged in destructive combat. The profoundest imagery in religion is used to point to the significance of goodwill among God's children. Even those who are professionally involved in the use of military power for the service of their countries think of themselves as primarily devoted to the preserving of peace. With rare exceptions, politicians promise to seek and to preserve peace, no matter how much they may think that arms are necessary for that purpose.

YEARNING FOR PEACE AND PREPARING FOR WAR

This wide, almost universal, yearning for peace stands in glaring contrast to ongoing realities in the world and to prevalent practices in political life. The nations continually prepare for war as a way of preserving their national rights and security. They make themselves poor in order to be strong. They seek to protect themselves by being able to threaten great harm to those who might attack them.

Military strength comes to be seen, not as something that deals in death and destruction, but as something to preserve national rights and security. Some nations, at least according to their professions, stockpile arms and raise armies in order to protect their friends as well as themselves. War Departments have long since become Defense Departments, and are concerned both for the protection of a nation's own security and that of its friends. So strongly do many people think of weaponry as a means to defend peace that some of them find little or no incongruity in naming a nuclear submarine *Corpus Christi*— the body of Christ.

Despite our attraction to peace as a hope, we routinely rely upon a system that regards war as a possibility and consider the capacity to wage war as the main, if not only, means to ensure peace. We consider defense expenditures to have a self-evident validity which no other governmental programs have. In our relationships with other nations we make matters of mutual security uppermost and define that security largely (if not only) in terms of military power. We have generally abandoned a simplistic isolationism that tries to avoid entangling involvements with other countries, but we have made our new involvements with the world more evident in military logistics than in imaginative diplomacy. We would be scandalized if our chief representative to a military alliance such as NATO were an officer critical of its performance and doubtful of its reason for being. But we have sent to the United Nations an ambassador who has those sorts of views about that organization. We begrudge even small contributions for the alleviation of hunger or injustice, either at home or abroad, but we have little hesitation (except perhaps in a severe budgetary crisis) about spending huge sums for the buildup of defense. Our Presidents do not hesitate to appear in the company of leaders of whatever nations put their might alongside our might in the alignment of international power, but they pointedly absent themselves from conferences of nations seeking to bring about disarmament. We give big scholarships or free expensive educations to those who will prepare themselves to lead our military forces, but we have little or no corresponding public support for those who would prepare for diplomatic service.

Yet with all this we still profess a concern about peace. We want to be considered a peace-loving people, not a warlike nation. We do homage to those who profess a concern about peace, and we honor with our lips both aspects of the advice ascribed to President Theodore Roosevelt, "Speak softly and carry a big stick." We never intend to use sticks—at least we never intend to be the first to use them. We have no doubts that we can be both strong and restrained, able both to "beat any kid-nation on the global street" and to remain the most benevolent and compassionate member of the international neighborhood. With sticks in our hands—yea, with guns in our arsenal and the remote-control buttons of missiles tingling at our fingertips—we still imagine that others see us as the epitome of soft-spoken benevolence.

Where are the influences that teach us how to speak softly? "Speaking softly" means more than rendering lip service to vague ideals. It means more than keeping a sullen quietness that may obscure a contempt for others' more demonic than noisy outbursts. To speak on behalf of peace is to communicate clearly and unmistakably that we are concerned for others as well as for ourselves. There is nothing in the possession of big sticks (or of even bigger bombs) that of itself instructs us how to speak profoundly about justice for others, freedom for all. There is very little about merely being strong that convinces others we have their welfare as our concern. We cannot build a peaceful world with a soft whimper where there ought to be an outcry for justice, or with a cowboy prowess and adventurism in our leaders when there ought to be maturity and compassion. We cannot build a peaceful world merely by ignoring those who are searching for a more equitable way to share in its benefits. If we trust mainly in the power we wield, and place no risk/hope in the achievement of mutuality with others in the business of global living, we will continue indefinitely in this yearning for peace while aggravating the conditions that make for conflict.

Christian piety contributes much to this widespread yearning for peace. The central place given to the idea of peace in the Bible elicits a widespread response in almost every Christian heart. But Christian behavior and practice has not been notably more effective in achieving peace than has been the behavior and practice of the world. When the church has exercised a major political influence, as it did in medieval Europe, its record at alleviating conflict has not been a commendable one. In many wars, some religious leaders have vehemently "presented arms" and a number still extol the mastery of military strength as the only way to achieve peace. It does not help merely to invoke religious piety on behalf of peace as long as our trust is in the instruments of war. We must come to see the Bible's vision of peace as the normative vision of God's intention for us and for other human beings.

PEACEKEEPING AS A VERSION OF WAR THINKING

Because we accept war as a seemingly inevitable part of human experience we think that peace can be kept by mastering the techniques of war. In this way we hope to protect ourselves (and help others to protect themselves) against those who would violate the territory, rights, or destinies of others. We may hope, a bit wistfully perhaps, that international sentiment can have a restraining effect on those who would do violence to peace, but we are unable to put much stock in the power of that sentiment to deter international wrongdoers from the wanton exercise of perverse intentions. Instead, we believe that only the capacity to visit swift and certain retribution against those who might do international mischief can provide any promise of keeping them from doing so. We persuade ourselves that the world is kept from chaos only by might.

Believing this, we easily think of military preparedness as a form of peacekeeping. Peacekeeping assumes that a threat to use armed violence (backed, of course, with the capacity to execute the threat and the resolve to do so if needed) is the chief hedge between ourselves and international outlawry. The intention to ensure peace by maintaining strength, to avoid war by being ready to fight it, is plausible to those whose idea of peace implies only the absence of actual violence. Armed truce has all the attributes of conflict except the overt killing. To force others to cower before a threat is not to achieve peace, even if (at least for a time) it prevents the outbreak of war. Peace maintained by the force of arms alone is a condition similar to that which Ezekiel condemned when he said of the citizens of his city, "They have misled my people, saying, 'Peace,' when there is no peace" (Ezek. 13:10a).

The logic of deterrence, while designed to keep peace, is essentially a logic of terror. Threats to use power to stop others from using their power do not get beyond a seesaw process that inevitably escalates the mastery of might—first on one side, then on the other. As the size of the threat on one side increases, often in an effort to counter the clout of the other side, the imagined need to increase military strength increases. Nations never rest assured that they are sufficiently strong to ensure that other nations cannot (or will not) challenge their strength. Peace-keeping by arms alone is based upon the use of fear. To live in fear is not to live in peace, but is at best only to live in hope for the absence of a destructive interchange with weaponry.

Moreover, to maintain a posture of deterrence requires us to think of another nation, or a group of nations, as enemies whose conduct cannot be changed by acts of persuasion. We tend to arm against other nations only when we are convinced we will not be safe unless we do. Our nerves get set on edge, not merely by the military threat we face, but by the belief that another nation seeks to do us in and will never work toward the solution of differences by negotiating or bargaining unless it fears our power. We mount arms against other nations to the extent we have concluded (and not always as a result of having tried to make them work) that no diplomatic initiatives, no efforts at cooperation, no gestures of goodwill, will ever be returned in good faith or lead to the solution of differences.

Peacekeeping by the mastery of military power over other nations does not of itself provide the ways or the inclination to reduce tensions or settle issues. When military concerns are accorded the main attention, political, economic, and diplomatic means to resolve disputes are frequently neglected. Instead of settling disagreements or working out the possibilities of coexistence with nations whose internal policies or ways of life are very different from ours, we simply make them so afraid of our might as to keep them at bay. Military power that is mounted merely as a bigger and bigger threat is qualitatively different from military power that is considered to be but one element in a broader pattern of national policy.

The stand-off atmosphere created by an arms race prompts the feeling that certain nations are so disruptive and dangerous that it will never be possible to live peace-

fully with them. But the fact is that we change relationships with other nations quite frequently. Those who lived
during the Second World War and heard Germany, Italy,
and Japan characterized as immutably evil seem quite
capable of looking upon them differently today. Years ago
Communist China was viewed as a massively large and
implacable enemy, and any suggestion that it would be
wise to recognize her diplomatically was considered tan-
tamount to treason. Many church groups were flagrantly
maligned for being soft on this matter. Today our attitude
toward a number of other countries that we consider left-
ish, or belligerent, is much like our attitude once was toward Red China. But if we can make great reversals of
attitude in one case, why must we consider it so impossible
to imagine that similar reversals might occur in other
cases?

Religion relates in various ways to a peacekeeping posture. One type of religious approach—best symbolized by
the baptized nationalism of a fervent minority—equates
the use of American military power with the doing of
God's will. This is a contemporary expression of the war
ethic of the crusade. A crusade ethic makes religious people more confident of their cause and self-righteous in its
pursuit than does a pragmatic approach to peacekeeping
as a terrible necessity in an unstable world. Crusaders look
upon enemies, not merely as threats to political security,
but as infidels and unbelievers, against whom it is imperative to use military power in the service of God's will. It
is curious that many of the same religious leaders who
decry how much America has wandered from her traditional reliance upon God and undergone moral decay still
identify the military strength of this country with the preservation of righteousness in the world. There is little impe-
tus to work for peace when the instruments of war make
possible moral heroics.

A religious embrace of peacekeeping can occur in much

more sensitive ways. Without identifying the interests of the nation with the will of God, many Christians acknowledge the need to use power, or the threat of power, to maintain tolerable balances between conflicting vitalities in a world that is infested with sin and prone to violence and conflict. Augustine gave the first theoretical foundation for this approach. He taught that Christians live in two realms: one, the heavenly city of God where peace is possible on the basis of reconciliation and love, and the other, the earthly city of ordinary politics where peace can be kept only by the use or threat of force. The Christian must never, as do crusaders, forget the difference between these two realms, yet may do what is necessary in the earthly city to keep the peace. The Christian will do this with a heart heavy about the dreadful necessity and with a deep regret over the condition of the world.

Martin Luther was somewhat more blunt about it. He suggested that Christians must respectfully obey the princes who rule the world even though they rightly realize that the princes are rogues and their exercise of power is a harsh, even cruel, enterprise rather than a loving achievement. Only the harshness of the princes holds back the flood of evil. Still, Luther never equated the work of the princes with the will of God.

The Augustinian way of dealing with these issues was strongly reflected in the thinking of Reinhold Niebuhr, which has influenced theology for almost half a century. Niebuhr spoke of the difference between moral man and immoral society, and argued that the kind of loving interchange possible on intimate levels cannot operate in the larger power relationships of political life. While Niebuhr's work, particularly in the later years of his life, did prompt him to subject the behavior of nations and empires to moral scrutiny, the general effect of this thinking was to find a way for Christians to legitimize the use of violence during the Second World War. In the late 1930s and early 1940s he prompted Americans to recognize the crisis in Europe, and many of his best-known works emerged from that effort.

The Second World War came to an end with the dropping of two atomic bombs, the destructive power of which exceeded by a quantum leap anything previously utilized in warfare. Soon after the dropping of the atomic bombs, the main ecumenical body in the United States, then called the Federal Council of Churches, gathered a group of theologians together to consider the issues posed by the unprecedented destructiveness that had become available for military purposes. Peacekeeping assumptions dominate the report of this group, which was entitled *The Christian Conscience and Weapons of Mass Destruction* and was issued in 1950. While this statement expressed alarm over the destructive capabilities of the new weapons, it reluctantly concluded there was no alternative but to build up the military and moral strength of the Western world with every kind of weapon. This report, and thinking like it, took the thinking that Reinhold Niebuhr developed to prompt American participation in the war itself and applied it to the postwar period. Alan Geyer, certainly no pacifist and a tough-minded advocate of international responsibility, has (from the standpoint of our present situation) judged this statement to amount to "a Cold War call to arms."[1]

The cold war that followed upon the heels of these events has seen the use of confrontational tactics carried to "peacetime" use far beyond anything that could have been imagined in 1950. It has been dominated by peacekeeping ways of thinking. Whereas after the First World War Americans were inclined to abandon reliance on military power as a means of keeping peace, after the Second World War they did a great deal to avoid that scenario. They kept up defenses against possible threats to peace, arguing only how big they needed to be. The nation set up a very large, seemingly permanent, military complex and super intelligence agency. It got involved in the Korean and Vietnam Wars because of peacekeeping ways of thinking applied on what has been a scale never previously known in American policy.

The Vietnam experience, however, produced a crisis of confidence. Many, including Reinhold Niebuhr, who were active in persuading Americans to assume a role in the European conflict in the 1940s became adamant opponents of the Vietnam War in the 1960s. But whereas in connection with intervention in Europe a compelling and impressive theological foundation was developed in Augustinian terms for the military necessities involved, there was little correspondingly extensive theological re-thinking done in connection with protests against the Vietnam War. Much of the current interest in peacemaking may well stem from the frustration that resulted from the adventure in Southeast Asia. A sanguine confidence in peacekeeping by the use of military power was shaken, but no alternative way of thinking has replaced it.

The frustration experienced in dealing with the Vietnam War, particularly the realization that international problems cannot be solved merely by hurling massive military might into a fray, has combined with an ever-escalating arms race to focus new attention on the problems of war and peace. The atomic arms race has emerged as nations have applied the same logic of deterrence to it as they traditionally applied to conventional weapons. The unprecedented dangers entailed have, along with the frustrations experienced in Vietnam, created a great interest in yet another approach to Christian thinking about war. The just war tradition, which seeks to specify the conditions under which it is legitimate to resort to war and to delineate the moral restraints upon strategies that may be used in war, has received a great deal of attention. The most recent instance of this is the effort of the American

Roman Catholic bishops to draft a pastoral letter on the moral issues of the nuclear arms race. This letter raises issues about the moral limits of peacekeeping, particularly about the legitimacy of applying the traditional justification for peacekeeping by military means to the unprecedented case of nuclear warfare. But, important as it has been, the work of the Catholic bishops did not move from war thinking to peace thinking. It has been more concerned with the moral problems posed by modern instruments of war than with how to achieve the conditions that make for peace.

WAR RESISTANCE AND WAR THINKING

The war in Vietnam produced a tremendous disillusionment in many circles with military solutions to international problems. At the same time, the unprecedented threat to existence itself posed by the nuclear arms buildup has raised grave doubts in many minds about the prudential usefulness of warfare as a means of keeping peace. These two developments have together produced an increasingly widespread resistance to war, which has become as evident in many places as pacifism became between the First and Second World Wars. Much discussion has developed about the importance of allowing conscientious objection to service in particular wars rather than to war in general.[2] This has intensified and broadened the discussion of war resistance.

War resisters hold that war is the enemy, that the preparations for war made in the name of peacekeeping merely intensify hostilities and lead to the very conflagrations they are designed to deter. War resisters believe that preoccupation with maintaining strength of arms against enemies poisons the international situation with distrust and polarizes the nations into armed camps. They point out that attempts to keep peace by power intensify hostility and bitterness and make us antagonistic toward any country that is not willing to make its destiny dependent upon our agenda.

Because arms races polarize the world and lead to the antagonisms from which war arises, military power must always be subject to critical moral scrutiny. Since such scrutiny comes so seldom from those committed to the bolstering of national strength, war resisters may have a special role to play—a role that seems to be one of "making war on warmaking." This role is not an easy one; it is subject both to miscasting and to misinterpretation. It may seem more preoccupied with stopping a rush to madness than with paving a way to reconciliation.

War resisters can alert us to the fact that victory with arms does not achieve peace. They can remind us that the buildup of strength can short-circuit diplomatic initiatives and efforts to remove the causes of conflict. War resisters can help us to remember that being strong can be as dangerous as being weak. War resisters are a valuable counterinfluence to those who think of peacekeeping only in terms of military power. Because they see military power as itself a problem and note how infrequently it achieves constructive results, they challenge the simplistic premise that military might is alone significant in determining the affairs of nations.

War resisters are important because they keep us acutely aware of the unconscious deference paid by so many people to the premises of violence and the primacy of power. They point out that preparation for war raises counterresponses that intensify the very antagonisms that thrive on power. If there were no war resisters, we might never question the contradictory premises that make us yearn for peace and prepare for war. We would go our merry way making truculence a virtue and thinking that safety can be assured by instruments of annihilation.

But war resistance, despite its contribution as a criticism

of war and a witness to the futility of conflict, lacks a procedural agenda for working toward peace. It does not, in and by itself, require us to work to establish the relationships in all areas of life on moral grounds. It can be content to withdraw from the prevalent evil. This is not a moral fault, but it can be a strategic shortcoming. To enunciate morality by condemning existing moral evil has a long and honorable heritage—starting with the Hebrew prophets. But the lives of people and the destinies of nations are prompted to more constructive achievement by a different craft. Those who would shepherd a society toward different postures and direct a people to the imaginative implementation of peacemaking must have more to offer. They must be able to teach us how to reconcile differences and establish justice, not merely warn of the counter-productivity of modern scientific violence and the futility of conflicts fought with it.

Toward Peace Thinking and Peacemaking

A peacemaker holds tenaciously to the belief that it is possible to reduce or to overcome the contrast between our yearning for peace and the reliance we place on war as a means of protecting human achievements. A peacemaker will believe, despite evidences to the contrary, that the relationships of human life—from those in closely covenanted groups up to and including those between nation-states—can be made consistent with moral purposes. To be sure, the means of communication and interaction differ between small and large groups. The problems in large groups may be greater and more difficult to deal with than those in small groups. But until we become concerned to bring the large and impersonal relationships of life under moral scrutiny just as we do the intimate ones, we will find the international tensions and suspicions we know all too well growing by leaps and bounds.

We do not find it difficult to accept the need to be morally sensitive and concerned for integrity within the personal relationships that exist in small and intimate groups. When dealing with others face-to-face we acknowledge the importance of being decent, of being concerned for the welfare and fortunes of others, of showing love and affection to immediate kin and close associates. Even the most vocal opponents of governmental aid to the needy are quite likely to respond humanely to individuals who approach them for assistance.

In the economic sphere, where relationships are less personalized, we still honor certain rules of the game. We may describe life in the marketplace as cutthroat, but woe to that enterpreneur who does not respect the agreed-upon procedures or honor the contractual obligations that govern commercial transactions. The most blatant, brutal, and unscrupulous pursuit of gain is curtailed when it is sought by means that are openly contemptuous of the procedural regularity that make operating trust possible in the business world. The commercial enterprise is possible only if competitiveness stops short of throat-slitting.

Every civilized society restrains within its borders behavior that violates the standards of a common covenant. Every civilized society thus bears witness, in its own way, to the importance of moral restraints and acknowledged proprieties in the relationships between persons and persons or between persons and groups. Some years ago, Americans were shocked when they learned that certain high government officials had used dirty tricks to manipulate the political process. The corruption that shocked the nation in the Watergate episode—unlike the petty corruption that is tolerated in political life on the ward level or in county courthouses—struck at the integrity of statecraft at its highest levels. Watergate revealed a corruption based upon a false belief that the exercise of a mighty office legitimizes the misuse of power, and that treachery and even deceit are appropriate ways of getting certain things done in connection with national security.

Watergate might not have occurred had those who were involved not learned dirty tricks by dealing with international intrigue. It is a small step from using techniques developed for the clandestine operations of the Central Intelligence Agency in other countries to protecting national security at home with similar methods. The tragedy of Watergate is that very few of those who were shocked when such techniques were employed in domestic affairs have reflected on the mischief played by the same practices when utilized in America's dealings with other peoples of the world.

A belief that relationships between persons and between groups must rest upon moral foundations is more the substance of an ideal than the fruit of an achievement. But human relationships, even in some very large settings, have frequently been brought under moral control and not left to be governed merely by coercive techniques implemented violently or by the threat of violence. In England, for instance, great pride has traditionally been taken in the fact that the public safety officers (that is, the bobbies) have not carried guns. Strong moral premises operate in English society and have enabled it, for a long and sustained period of time, to maintain law and order without having to maximize the devices of coercion. Unarmed police, as many other cherished expressions of justice and order, may become things of the past in England. If they disappear, that will be a tragedy more than it will be a proof that English society was "unrealistic" in expecting to control civic life without guns. When only violence, or the threat of violence, can compel submission to civil order, something very significant is missing from a society.

Not many nations can boast of England's (not temporary, we hope) achievement. America cannot. The presence of coercive violence as a means of maintaining public order lies far closer to the surface of our common life than it does to the surface of civic life in England. To the extent that this is the case we are less a peaceful society. Unfortunately, much of our popular thinking has encouraged a myth that unofficial watchers of law and morality—like lone rangers—are more effective than sheriffs or other law-enforcement officials in maintaining things aright. If we gave as much attention to holding officials to moral standards, and treating them with the esteem to elicit such standards, as we do to making heroes out of charismatic private operators, we might have a better public justice in our midst.

In contrast to many places in the world, where graft is normal and corruption rampant, America does have a large residual integrity, respect for order, and concern for domestic tranquillity. Yet when these erode or seem to slip, we often respond with demands to escalate the instruments of coercive control—to let the police really clobber criminals—rather than with an attempt to refurbish public commitment to the moral foundations of human interaction. Perhaps there are two Americas—one which believes that civil order is possible on moral foundations and the other which believes that only the threat of violence keeps thugs off the streets and thieves from the door. Americans can be heard arguing, sometimes at one and the same time, that peace and order are essential to national well-being and also that every citizen needs to own arms for self-protection.

But the most crying need of the present time is not to overcome the split consciousness in the American spirit but to tackle an even more serious degree of suspicion between the nations. The use of warfare as a means to keep peace has become increasingly precarious and potentially suicidal. We simply cannot continue to rely upon ever-escalating armaments, coupled with a growing cynicism about the prospects of bringing international order under a semblance of moral control, to make the future secure or attractive. We must change our ways of thinking, and our ways of acting. This will be a momentous task, perhaps far more difficult than anything we have recently done as a people.

The urgency is obvious in the case of nuclear armaments. George Kennan, whose credentials as a political realist are without blemish, contends that nuclear weapons simply cannot be employed in a politically responsible way, and therefore that thinking which depends upon their possible use for deterrent purposes simply has to be repudiated. He writes, "The public discussion of the problems presented by nuclear weaponry which is now taking place in this country is going to go down in history . . . as the most significant that any democratic society has ever engaged in."[3]

We welcome Kennan's witness, and plead for a still more extensive agenda. We must probe to the very assumptions that prevent a culture from trusting in peaceful responses and we must remake our very soul as a people. We must articulate foundational convictions and develop theoretical understandings that can replace those which can no longer serve us well. The task is as confounding as it is compelling, but no fear of failure or feeling of inadequacy should allow us to withdraw from the arduous effort and the risks of faith that are involved. We have to learn how to think about peace. And we cannot, and dare not, rule out in advance the contributions, however divergent or vexing they may be, of any persons or groups that bring good faith and an open spirit to this task.

II

From Retribution to Creative Justice

It is impossible to think about peace without thinking about justice. There can be no genuine peace in human affairs unless individuals and groups are treated properly and fairly by others, and in turn feel themselves obliged to treat others with respect and righteousness. Justice is a broad and marvelous concept, but we often fail to think of it creatively. We must put away limiting and inadequate ways of thinking about justice and come to understand it as the foundation of community and as the precondition of that harmonious interaction needed for peace.

SOME INADEQUATE THINKING ABOUT JUSTICE

We often think of justice as a system of protecting people from harm. We associate justice with the means of enforcement that get, or try to get, people to do things or to behave in ways that they would not out of mere goodwill. If unruly types threaten the civil order, we call the police and engage the prosecutors in order "to bring them to justice." If a person fails to abide by the rules of the state, for example, speeding on the highway, failing to pay taxes, deliberately writing bad checks, or shoplifting, we expect that person to "face the bar of justice" and to be punished if found guilty. If people take undue advantage of others and seem to benefit illegitimately from dishonest dealings, we often comment to the effect that they should get the "just due" of their behavior.

Punitive, retributive, and scolding elements often dominate such thinking about justice. While we know in theory that a system of justice must be as fully concerned to vindicate the innocent as to accuse the guilty, in our ordinary responses we say "that person got justice" only in cases of conviction and punishment. In contrast, if acquittal is involved, we say something like that person "beat the rap," or "got off the hook," or "sure was lucky." Or again, whereas we say of those whose actions have been socially disruptive that "they should be given justice," we seldom say of those whose behavior has been remarkably fair and generous in relating to others that they have "exemplified justice at its finest."

Justice, as we most commonly think of it, adjudicates claims, redresses grievances, protects the majority from socially destructive behavior, and legitimizes means of defense against danger or exploitation. In these functions justice is enforced by authority and depends upon some level of coercion. The state steps in to settle conflicts between parties under its jurisdiction. It can do so because it can enforce its decisions. Justice as understood in this way is, in the terms of Luther, "a dyke against sin." It fulfills the protective function of keeping human life orderly and reasonably secure.

This way of thinking about justice as an exercise in power which keeps disorder from running rampant through the political sphere is even more prevalent in our thinking about international affairs than in our assumptions about the domestic order. Indeed, relationships between nations are often thought to be governed more by force, or the threat of force, than relationships between persons or the interaction between smaller groups in a healthy society. When states conflict with other states, each often claims that its cause is "just" and that its resort to the use of violence is the only way it can protect or obtain that which it believes itself to be entitled. There are a few international arrangements available for the adjudication of claims by other means, but the scope of such arrangements (like the World Court) is very limited. Most differences that really matter are settled by the threat of force or the use of force. Paul Ramsey, speaking of how issues are settled in wartime, once put the matter bluntly: "In politico-military conflict you cannot win at the conference table anything that *it is evident* you cannot win or are *not resolved to win* on the battlefield."[4]

What Ramsey holds to be true about wartime circumstances, many others have come to think is the case in all international relationships. Richard Rubenstein, a forthright and cogent interpreter of cultural realities, has not hesitated to state the problem bluntly. Believing that ethical ideals have lost much of their power to restrain people to a search for harmonious interaction, at least in affairs between nation-states, Rubenstein has stated conceptually what many assume operationally.

> In the confrontations between nations, radical conflicts of interest can only be resolved on the basis of power relationships. No other basis is credible. This does not mean that every conflict must be resolved by the use of all available power. It does mean that, short of an actual conflict, a nation's power in international conflict will largely be determined by the estimate her adversaries have of that power. All we have left to preserve some measure of peace is a balance of mutual nuclear terror. At the very least the great powers are condemned to an inextricable cycle of ever-widening arms races, especially as

weapons systems achieve ever greater sophistication.
It is my belief that there is no way out of this bind.[5]

When understood in these retributive ways, justice is closely and inextricably linked with conflict. Even when nations do not go "all out" to protect their interests (or the interests of others) by the threat or the use of force, they assume that any weakness on their part will open them, and those with whom their destiny is interlaced, to exploitation or to blackmail. Justice is considered to be related to strength and considered to depend upon the willingness to maintain and to employ the means of coercion for the protection of things to which nations believe themselves entitled. While not always so baldly stated, this way of thinking has been a central assumption of political realism in every historical epoch and in most places on the globe.

When thinking about justice moves along the lines indicated, it is quite difficult to avoid a conclusion that says, in effect, "Only the threat of force can implement or ensure justice." Practically speaking, we then operate on an assumption that peaceful ways of relating to one another are nice conveniences in incidental diplomacy, but that when things really count we must trust in the means of war as the only reliable safeguard of social order. A chaplain in the Second World War became famous for exemplifying such realism. When his prayers and pastoral ministrations failed, he took a place on the ramparts in a moment of desperation, and sang, "Praise the Lord, and pass the ammunition."

JUSTICE AS EQUALITY AND FAIRNESS

To warrant identification as a peacemaker requires that we refuse to think of the human situation as governable only by terror. There are sound appraisals of human life which do not cave in to a reductionistic belief that the only operable and viable forms of human action are those which outclaw the jungle. It is not utopian, it is not unrealistic, to think of justice as a set of conditions that significantly enhances human action, that makes possible human community at all levels, and that creates circumstances in which persons and groups feel sufficiently well treated to cooperate for mutual benefit and to support each other for agreed-upon purposes.

If any of us had a family of several children, we would expect domestic tranquillity only if we treated all our children with reasonable fairness. We would anticipate difficulty if we showered great affection or disproportionate benefits on one or two siblings and deprived the others of love and material support. Of course, we might "keep the peace" in an unfair household by a harsh exercise of coercive discipline, but such a state of affairs would not be an enviable one.

To work for conditions of fairness requires great skill and imagination. No simplistic, quantifiable, equalitarianism suffices. There are many variables, even in a family of very similar people and almost identical fortune, that must be weighed and evaluated in seeking to be fair. For instance, an older sibling—say, in high school—has more needs and is therefore entitled to a higher allowance than a younger one. A handicapped child may well require higher medical outlays and more helping attention than the normally robust one. Emotional needs may vary, and warrant different kinds, even different degrees, of attention. For these differentiations to be acceptable, all members of the family will have to be persuaded that such differentiations are legitimate expressions of love seeking to be just. They may not always be immediately or totally accepted as just, but unless their credibility is established among all who are affected by them, there is not likely to be tranquillity in the household.

Just as differentiations may be legitimized on the basis of need, within reasonable bounds they may also be legitimized on the basis of reward. The member of a family who does something unique—such as win a contest of skill, achieve a particularly good report from school, prove especially thoughtful in an act of charity or helpfulness, or earn money through diligent dedication to some productive work performed in lieu of idleness—may well deserve special recognition. Often these achievements bring their own returns, and it is unnecessary to supplement those with added accolades. Differentiations stemming from achievement are always part of human experience. The trick is to allow them to be incentives to achievement without becoming occasions of envy or division between people who ultimately have more in common than they differ in worth. A parent who gave a thousand dollars to the child with an A-minus school average and put the one with a B-plus average out of the house would be a very unjust parent indeed. In the end, even the prodigal son, who squandered all he was due in a life of rebellion and bad judgment, was welcomed home by the father. The elder brother, who thought such forgiveness to be unfair, had a point—but by allowing it to get full sway over his thinking he actually cut himself off from the father's love.

There are two faces of justice: the one that emphasizes equality of treatment to all who belong in a given family or community and the other that emphasizes the importance of rewarding extraordinary achievement with appropriate differentiations. It is difficult to reconcile these, or to create a viable community if only one of them is taken into account. We find both approaches portrayed in the New Testament, the first in the parable of the vineyard workers who all got the same pay regardless of the hour they reported for work, and the other in the parable of the talents, in which people were praised for achieving in proportion to their resources. In contrast to the treatment of the prodigal son, we have the phrase of Paul (so dear to entrepreneurial types): "If any one will not work, let that person not eat" (I Thess. 3:10).

We find these same two faces of justice in philosophical thinking. The equalitarian dimensions of justice figure more predominantly in the thinking of John Rawls[6]; the dimensions of proportionate rewards and the freedom to pursue them, in that of Robert Nozick.[7] The incentive dimension is the most professed aspect of capitalist theory and the equality/need dimension that of Communist theory, but neither creates a system in which only one dynamic is operative. Both must wrestle with the problem of keeping the claims of equality in tension with the place of incentives.

These considerations do not relate merely to economic goods. Indeed, disproportionate distributions of economic goods may not be the most insidious kinds of injustice people can experience. Many conditions have prevented and still prevent fairness and justice from blossoming on earth like the lilies of the field. For instance, a considerable differentiation was once commonplace in the treatment of the male or female members of the family. This distinction was not merely functional—girls getting baby dolls and boys, cowboy guns—but extended to things like educational opportunity, inheritance distributions, and other privileges. We now know there can be no peace in households where such distinctions persist. We are also coming to realize that there can be no peace in a community or in a world that does not overcome such arbitrary inequalities in the older customs.

Similarly, we have experienced—or, more precisely, are undergoing—a changing perception about justice in relationship to coloration of skin. At one time the unexamined assumption about Anglo-Saxon superiority was strong enough to legitimize an institution as unjust, barbaric, and tragic as slavery. It is difficult for many today to imagine how this could have been the case. Yet, the overt and covert racism that exists in practically every part of the globe is too little recognized. Even the most open-minded and well-intended of those who belong to the Caucasian minority are victims of an unrecognized tendency to think of our own kind as different (and in unexpressed ways, as "better") than those of other ethnic identities. This legacy has bitter consequences in our nation and in the world. It lies behind serious continuing economic differentiations, segregated housing patterns, differences in educational opportunity and social mobility, and a host of subtle injustices that those of us who live in privileged circumstances simply do not sense.

There can be no peace unless those customs and pre-judgmental biases that exacerbate inequality on the basis of things like sex and race are overcome. And who of us knows which customs today that tacitly legitimize differentiations will not, from the perspective of the future, be seen to be just as arbitrary, just as illegitimate, and just as conducive to rancor as those which are now coming to be recognized as in need of immediate and complete overhaul? We must live in a continual sensitivity to every differentiation that is accepted without challenge, lest we sow the seeds of discontent for those who come after us and have to be judged to be as blind to the injustices under our very noses as those who before us seem to have been blind to injustice in the midst of their experience.

JUSTICE BETWEEN NATIONS

Larger human relationships are subject to the same dynamics. Unfairness in the acquisition, possession, and control of those resources which support, and those privileges which enhance, the quality of life is a root cause of conflict. People of the world no longer accept the premise that opportunity belongs only to a certain pigmentation of the skin, or that the destiny of those in the so-called Third and Fourth Worlds should be determined by the affluence of the superpowers. A few nations cannot have, nor can special groups within nations have, a great preponderance of the benefits of life on this planet without becoming causes of rancor. Inevitably, underresourced nations will protest the oppressive conditions under which they have been forced to live. As long as unfairness in the enjoyment of the earth's resources is great there will be conflict no matter how piously we yearn for peace or think of ourselves as dedicated to it. Until we come to think of justice as a condition of reasonable common enjoyment of the earth's resources, we can expect wars and rumors of war to continue.

It is important to realize that the world has, until quite recently, been spared the backlash that comes when unfairness prevails. This is so because several conditions have enabled injustice to persist without being keenly felt. These circumstances can be described by the rubric "distance." This term covers such factors as geographical separation and cultural isolation. If people are so separated from one another as not to interact—not to be aware of their condition vis-à-vis that of others—they do not experience a sense of injustice even if their condition warrants outrage. Many people have supposed that modern means of communication will do much to bring the peoples of the world together—to make the whole world a neighborhood. They have supposed that the shrinking of geographical distances and removal of cultural isolations would contribute to a greater human solidarity. But the truth of the matter is that this will happen only if justice prevails. If faster and more adequate communication only reveals to the dispossessed and to the oppressed how badly they fare and how much their plight contrasts with the freedom and affluence others enjoy, the result will be to exacerbate the conditions of conflict rather than to create the possibilities of peace. The technological elimination of distance will result in community only if accompanied by a corresponding increase in justice.

Another form of "distance" is secrecy. In a family unit, for instance, a parent can possibly give one child among the others some special and undeserved favor by saying, "This is just between us, don't tell your sisters or brothers about it!" This sometimes works for a little while, but often it backfires as the truth comes out. Secrecy can seldom cover injustice indefinitely, and when the plot is uncovered there are two resentments to deal with instead of one: the injustice itself and the attempt to cover it up.

Attempted secrecy can lead to trouble in close or intimate relationships; it also leads to trouble in larger contexts. We may be tempted to think that it is possible to make secret concordats and "deals" between nations because the distances between them are great and the interactions highly impersonal. But that ignores the communications revolution. We increasingly live in an international goldfish bowl, and covert operations are increasingly likely to be recognized. They will become openly known in countries with a free press and free broadcasting systems, and known through the grapevine process that works so intensely in other situations. Informational "distance" provides less and less a way to hide injustice in the modern world.

In the past, inequalities have often been accepted as accidents of history. Some siblings are beautiful, others ugly; some nations have many natural resources, others do not. These differences are not due to any act or decision made by those involved, or even by those who have benefited from them, but are "given" by accidents of fortune over which there has been no direct human control. But modern civilization has nurtured a tendency to see fewer and fewer things as "acts of God." As we have increased our presumed control over natural events, and to a lesser extent over historical events, less and less credibility can be attached to fortuitous inequalities, and less and less patience is present to put up with them indefinitely. One of the prices—if it is a "price"—of acquiring an increased knowledge and expanded skills in dealing with natural and social surroundings is the fact that people are no longer patient with injustices that have no direct source in human agency and cannot be traced to deliberate culpability.

To be sure, accidentally inflicted inequalities will be a part of our experience until the created world and human history are redeemed in the final culmination of the divine purpose. Meanwhile, the parameters of differentiation that can be legitimized by appealing to the accidental fortunes of nature and history are shrinking. We are no longer prone to confine any persons or peoples to a condition of gross disadvantage with the simple excuse that they happen to be unlucky. The wheels of justice grind ever more finely and with increased expectations of fairness to all, and they can be expected to do so to an ever-increasing extent with the passage of time. It cannot be otherwise in a world providentially influenced by a God whose very nature is to be concerned for the outcast, and even for the sinner. There is no religious vision worthy of respect that thinks of human history as culminating in a condition of magnified inequality—the rich getting richer and the poor getting poorer. Isaiah's vision of the new age was one in which the valleys are lifted up and the mountains made low. Only under such conditions can the glory of the Lord be revealed and all flesh see it together (Isa. 40:4a, 5a).

JUSTICE, FAITH, AND RISK

Between the punitive and the creative attitudes toward justice sketched in this chapter, the second is most in harmony with the biblical understanding of the term. The quality of justice in God is related to his saving, not merely his judgmental functions, and is consistent with, rather than antithetical to, such other attributes as love, mercy, and faithfulness. As Professor John R. Donahue has said, "Justice is not simply the quality of God as righteous judge over sinful [persons], but a relation of the saving power of God to a world captured by evil. God's justice is his fidelity which inaugurates a saving victory over the powers that enslave and oppress [us]."[8] Waldron Scott, an evangelical Protestant, uses the term "rectification" to refer to the biblical understanding of God's work in turning the world toward a justice that sets social and economic conditions aright.[9] When we truly decide to do justice, we must decide not so much to become tough and harsh as to embody qualities of mercy, of love, and of concern for all the children of God. Amos wrote, "Let justice roll down like waters, and righteousness like an ever-flowing stream" (Amos 5:24). He did not suggest that in order to be just we must forget about mercy, or that in order to be responsible we have to master the techniques of power.

If we can let our actions and policies be shaped by a creative rather than a defensive/coercive vision of justice, certain changes might eventuate in the way we relate to one another in all the circumstances of life. These changes cannot suddenly alter the dynamics of human interaction into sweetness and light overnight. We must expect a long, costly, steady process of seeking to relate to others on the basis of empathy for their predicament, concern for their aspirations, appreciation of their yearnings, and a sometimes painful honesty in communicating with them. This isn't easy; it can be costly; and it will have as many failures and heartaches attached to it as do the other efforts we make to deal with the rough and tough realities of human affairs.

But if we take seriously the demands of creative justice, we will relocate our willingness to take risks. There are

risks in every path we choose. Any effort to treat other
nations fairly, seeking to extend them an initiative of trust,
believing that it may be better to undo an injustice we
have caused than to mount a force to prevent an injustice
they may do, is very risky.

We have become accustomed by many years of political
behavior to live with the risks that are entailed in seeking
national security by the use of power. We become ac-
climated to higher and higher risks as the weapons of
destruction become more and more powerful and capable
of more rapid deployment. In the Confession of 1967 The
United Presbyterian Church U.S.A. said that the search for
cooperation and peace also requires us to take risks. Such
a search "requires that the nations pursue fresh and responsible relations across every line of conflict, even at risk
to national security, to reduce areas of strife and to
broaden international understanding." There was some
heated discussion about that sentence when it was first
proposed, revealing that a number of people were deeply
disturbed by the idea of risk-taking for peace. These same
people, however, seem quite ready to support risk-taking
for war. As a people we need to help officials know that we
will support them if they are willing to venture for creative consequences in the political sphere as much as or
more than we support them when they take risks in conventional ways.

Likewise, we shall have to sacrifice. We now do so in
order to maintain huge military arsenals and to deploy
them around the world. Fiscal conservatives, although
they abhor deficit spending and will not do it for the alleviation of human misery at home or abroad, add to the
national debt in order to purchase armaments. This does
not eliminate the element of sacrifice but postpones the
reckoning for future generations to face. While defense
budgets escalate (and even skyrocket with cost plus over-
runs!), programs that might alleviate misery on an interna-

tional scale are not given sufficient place in our budgets. In early 1983, Secretary of State George P. Shultz, faced with the fact that Congress had not enacted a foreign-aid appropriations bill for two previous years, attempted to rally support for building up the economic well-being of regions in the world necessary to our security. He cited some comparisons that show how reluctant we are to help even friendly countries who need it. The total cost of the proposed aid came to $43.81 a person, about a tenth of what we had spent for armaments in 1980. Americans currently spend $104 a person for television and radio sets, $35 for services at barbershops and beauty parlors, $97 for soap and cleaning supplies, and $21 for flowers and potted plants. The Secretary of State didn't put his figures alongside those being used by the Secretary of Defense in asking for appropriations with which to buy weapons. Had he done so, the ratio for 1983 would have shown up to be $17 for guns and bombs for every dollar for aid. By 1986, if the growth rate in defense spending is continued and foreign aid held constant, the ratio will be 25 to 1.

We say that giveaways have not purchased peace. It is like the owner of a million-dollar estate who complains that nickels distributed to the poor at Christmastime do not eliminate poverty. A concern for justice consistent with the search for peace will transform this paltry, selfish concern about resources. It will refuse to settle blandly for the continuation of indifference. It will condemn the protection of privilege that results in such violence to human dignity as quietly takes place through the present ordering of priorities.

Finally, if we are impelled by a creative vision of justice, we will base our relationships to others on different grounds. As it is, we tend to trust and associate with only those people who adopt our scheme of things. In the world we befriend those who are against the same groups we are against. We ask only whether or not they will be enemies of our enemies, not whether they will share our hopes for freedom, our sense of fairness, or a concern for the alleviation of human needs. We choose our allies, not as do close associates and companions in noble causes, but as outlaws choose confederates in intrigue—people to use in a quest for strategic victory over some other party. There are always enough other nations willing to play such roles, particularly if we wink at their foibles, ignore their immoralities, and bolster their internal injustices as long as they side with us in a power game.

It has been said that to reverse such ways of doing things is to be utopian, to embrace an idealistic approach in a realm in which scruples do not fit, to wish for a world that ought to be rather than to relate to a world that is. There may be some truth in this. It is important to know that the world abounds in evil and bad faith, to realize that the innocent may be fleeced if they are not shrewdly tough, to appreciate that weakness can invite disaster, and to be aware that the mere profession of ideals does not change the behavior of others. But unless we argue for something more than a sophisticated contention that we have to deal with the world in the very same way those whose behavior we most abhor deal with it, what are we doing more than they are doing? Unless our sense of justice exceeds that of the cynics and the calculating realists, how can we build the peaceable kingdom?

III

From Repression
to Ordered Freedom

There is little chance of having genuine peace unless people are treated justly and are convinced that they are being treated justly. But justice does not come about as a casual accident. The interactions between people must be governed. The dynamics within any social unit—from family to nation-state—must be deliberately arranged and monitored in order to achieve communal well-being. Peace, therefore, depends upon how wisely and skillfully we shape and nurture the life of the groups to which we belong. Doing this well depends upon being clear about what we intend to accomplish and how we will overcome the obstacles that get in the way of social well-being.

THE KINSHIP OF FREEDOM AND ORDER

Two concepts help us to think about the governing of human affairs. Philosophers and theologians have wrestled at length with these two concepts, and political leaders have frequently faced the problem of balancing them. One of these concepts is the idea of freedom—an idea that gives wide latitude to the desires, wishes, and legitimate concerns of the individual. The other idea is the idea of order—an idea that points to the conditions under which individuals can creatively interact because they willingly accept certain restraints on their wants and behavior.

Neither of these ideas can operate in a society to the exclusion of the other without serious consequences for the general welfare. If freedom is maximized, social order can suffer because persons (or social subgroups) do their own thing without regard for how their behavior affects others. If order is maximized, freedom suffers because those who are in control—whether by official designation or the manipulation of power—often harshly repress any transgression of their will.

We can learn about these matters by looking at the political side of biblical experience. Ancient Israel went through many episodes that illustrate the difficulties of balancing freedom and order. During the periods when the loosely confederated tribes of Israel were ruled by charismatic leaders, the writer of The Book of Judges put the problem succinctly: "In those days there was no king in Israel; every man did what was right in his own eyes" (Judg. 17:6). Because this caused problems, the people of Israel came to feel that more order should be provided by the establishment of a hereditary monarchy.

There was a debate about this both before and after it happened. The writer of Jotham's fable (Judg. 9:7–15) was among those who clearly were displeased with the establishment of the monarchy and felt that it created greater order at too high a price. There was a price. Kings like David and Ahab, among others, used their offices, not only to bring the nation together and give it stability, but to satisfy their personal wishes and ambitions. For example, David stealthily took the wife of Uriah the Hittite (see II Sam. 11:2–27) and Ahab, through the malicious machinations of Jezebel, misappropriated Naboth's vineyard (I Kings 21:1–14). In both instances prophets directly challenged the misuses of power and both kings repented of the wrong they had done. That such challenges could occur and were effective shows that, even though the monarchy in Israel had increased order, it had not done so at the complete expense of freedom. Would that all subsequent exercises of authority in the name of protecting order could have been similarly subject to the free exercise of prophetic criticism!

In the New Testament we find two attitudes. In one place we see a recognition that publicly established authority (as exemplified by the Roman state) is a crucial protector of order. In another place we sense deeply held feelings that the exercise of authority can be a demonic enemy of faith and freedom. In Romans 13, Paul contends that rulers who maintain order are ordained by God for our protection against evildoers. He tells us to give them unqualified, or almost unqualified, obedience. In Revelation 13, the beast (with a coded designation pointing to the Roman emperor) is portrayed as the enemy of faith and of the freedom of Christians to follow their own consciences and way of life. They are warned to have nothing whatever to do with him. Both of these passages are responses to circumstances experienced by their authors: Paul enjoyed the protection of the Pax Romana when he was writing his epistle; the writer of Revelation saw great persecution of the Christian movement. The contrast between Romans 13 and Revelation 13 should help us to see how important it is to be concerned about both freedom and order and to recognize the possible errors into which we can fall if we try to deal with human affairs in terms of only one of them.

The tendency to establish order to a neglect of freedom has been repeated many times in Christian history. The medieval church was prone to place a priority on authoritatively maintained order, and the popes frequently became as powerful and as corrupt as the emperors. Luther, even though he rebelled against the medieval church on many matters, was just as prone as it had been to believe that order is prior to freedom. Inspired by Romans 13 he admonished his followers to be obedient to the princes by whose exercise of power his reformation movement was protected. He was particularly severe in his hostility to the peasants who revolted against the existing order and the injustices which they experienced under it.

In a memorable and classic chapter in *The Brothers Karamazov*, entitled "The Grand Inquisitor," Fyodor Dostoevsky has examined very pointedly why a pressure to embrace order to the exclusion of freedom often arises in human life. The cardinal who wields the power of the church confronts the Christ figure who refuses to play the power role and even dares to suggest that it was foolish for Christ to reject the temptation to use bread as an instrument of social control. "No science," he observed, "will give them bread so long as they remain free. In the end they will lay their freedom at our feet, and say to us, 'Make us your slaves, but feed us.' "[10] In describing the mind-set of the cardinal, who conducts the hunt for the heretics endangering the order established by the church, the character Alyosha says:

> He claims it as a merit for himself and his Church that at last they have vanquished freedom and have done so to make men happy. "For now" (he is speaking of the Inquisition, of course) "for the first time it has become possible to think of the happiness of men. Man was created a rebel; and how can rebels be happy?"[11]

A political scientist-theologian who lived in Germany during the rise of Hitler has described how conditions there also showed that people will give up their freedom for something to eat. Speaking of the situation in Germany, he observed how, "as democratic society disintegrates in the social and economic crisis, the people, fearing starvation and civil war, throw away their liberty and turn to Fascism for the restoration of order. What free people cannot achieve in freedom, they now call upon the use of force to achieve."[12]

Many Americans have enough bread and enough security so that they think mainly of the importance of freedom. But we who fancy that we have the moral vision to behave differently from people who give in to totalitarianism in order to eat, or to an authoritarian church in order to assure heavenly bread, dare not congratulate ourselves too glibly. Many of us are willing to lay our freedom at the feet of those who can provide order. We willingly submit to luggage and body scans before boarding planes because by doing so we can be spared the threat of hijacking in the sky. If muggings and robberies increase in the areas around our home, we accept curfews and private patrols to alleviate our anxiety. If robberies or rip-offs take place in the situations in which we work, we reluctantly submit to the use of lie detectors or other probes into the private lives of employees as the price of keeping a job. Who among us, member of a business concern, working in an academic institution, holding appointment based upon political affiliation, is not tempted to tailor our behavior to the imagined wishes of those who hold our paycheck (or our merit raises) in their power? If internal subversion becomes a real or imagined threat, we may tolerate the creation of special forces and even advocate the suspension of constitutionally protected liberties in order to secure the state against potential harm.

So, it is true that order, which includes all those processes that make life possible, is important for living. Without order life becomes desperate and even unbearable, and people will succumb to leadership that promises to fulfill their needs. But the reverse situation can also occur. It is possible that people, particularly under conditions of repression, can be persuaded to forget about the importance and value of order and to look only for emancipation from restraints and obligations.

Whenever political and social order becomes so rigid and so oppressive as totally to preclude the possibility of amelioration by any moderating forms of political action, the tendency of people to forget about the importance of order in the quest for freedom becomes very great. Oppressive conditions that stifle or inhibit people from having what they legitimately need or doing what they legitimately want to do create a great pressure to seek freedom without being concerned about order. Unfortunately, in many places in the contemporary world, horrendously repressive regimes present people with such a pressure. All discussion of change is outlawed, all efforts to ameliorate injustices are stifled, all forms of voluntary association are banned, and all human aspirations to be treated fairly are ridiculed or snuffed out by the use of intrigue, internal informers, and even torture. It is no wonder that people living under such conditions place the priority on the quest for freedom instead of on the institutionalized ordering of life. Moreover, it is noteworthy that the very Roman Catholic Church that in the medieval situation produced grand inquisitors to protect order is in our time, in places where there is great political and economic hardship, currently producing people and priests who are in the forefront of liberation movements.

Because the predicament of so many poor nations is so severe, and the repression so great, liberation thought has a momentous appeal in the contemporary world. Peoples who are living in the "Egypts" of these times—under conditions of oppression amounting to a kind of slavery—know why the exodus is such a primary and powerful symbol in biblical experience. The liberation theme has tremendous power in those places where the dominant political order maintains control by eliminating all challenges to official policy and thwarting every possibility of freely advocating changes to overcome poverty and exploitation.

It is easy to suppose that such conditions are typical of places beyond our influence or control. But there are those within America's borders who feel systematically barred from the benefits of living here. They are also interested in liberation—in liberation from overt and even more pervasive covert forms of exclusion that affect them. Denied equal access to housing, similar education, parallel job opportunity, and the enjoyments of a life-style known by most other Americans, these people also dream of freedom. Their plight may not seem so desperate as that of persons in other lands. Our Government has (at least in the past) tried to order our common life toward justice. Many of our moral prophets have emphasized the need for inclusion of all persons in the social order. But the vision lags and the exclusion persists and it would be no wonder, if conditions are not improved, to see people come to doubt a system that "does them out." A freedom that allows a majority to exclude a minority is little better than an order that allows a minority to oppress the majority.

This analysis may also help us to understand why, once revolutionary movements gain power or control (that is, become responsible for ordering life and providing bread), they often behave much as did the repressive regimes which they displaced. If there are few, if any, established patterns of responsibility and procedure, the chances of having the fruits of freedom are very slim. It takes years to build the fabric of common concern and social responsiveness that make it possible for a society to function with a balance between freedom and order.

FREEDOM AND ORDER IN THE WORLD SITUATION

How do these dynamics apply to the current situation in the world? The most prevalent condition among the many nations in the Third World is one in which great masses have neither freedom nor bread. Therefore, they do not barter away freedom in order to get bread as much as they have to decide which to seek first. They have little freedom within the political systems that exist in their own countries or protection from the power of the countries right around them; they have equally little hope of "bread" (or, of a significantly fruitful and productive kind of "order") from the economic conditions under which they live. One of the great powers provides them with an ideology that says in effect that if they will choose freedom, bread will follow; the other great power tells them to choose bread and then freedom will follow—if not right away, after the new kind of order is completely entrenched.

We ignore everything that Dostoevsky has suggested about how people act, and much about the ways we ourselves act, if we think that the promise of freedom alone will be persuasive to them. People will be attracted to bread rather than to freedom as long as the scheme under which they are living leaves them hungry, fearful of disorder, or uncertain about the prospects of life itself. We can decry this fact; we can preach that it should be otherwise; we can argue that those who are abjectly hungry or totally unprotected by the political situation in which they find themselves should (out of some idealism persuasive to us) act as we should like to think they should act rather than how the Grand Inquisitor said they will act. As long as we do so, however, our chance to nurture a creative interface between freedom and order in the experience of other nations will flounder.

Our own experience as a country is both a help and a source of confusion about this. Americans were once in a situation in which they had to choose between order and freedom and they made a clear choice for freedom. This leads them to think that others should do likewise. But to think this way is to ignore the conditions that made it easier for Americans to choose freedom centuries ago than it is for people to do so today. Americans were fortunate to be in a geographical setting of many natural resources that enabled them to produce "bread" enough while enjoying freedom. They were fortunate to be starting something anew rather than trying to remake a situation in which all the vested interests of the old regime were still powerful. They did not have other nations profiting from the economic exploitation of their goods and services— befriending and supporting an existing oppressive regime in order to keep the trade channels of commerce lucrative. Economic needs were simpler, and could be satisfied on a more frugal level than is likely today. The young nation had a relatively homogeneous background and a far greater consensus about the meaning and purpose of political institutions than is present in many places today, and it could initiate and secure its venture without interference from the other side of the oceans. While it was still protected from outside exploitation, our nation gained sufficient strength to weather the strains and stresses that have subsequently been put upon it.

But we must not be fooled. We cannot expect that other nations less blessed with resources and less protected from interference, can reenact our experience. If we think that only freedom needs to be sought, then we will fail to understand the way people will embrace even repressive order when the price of cherishing freedom is abject hunger. Many people like to repeat, "Give me liberty or give me death!" But these words mean something different to a relatively comfortable people, who might risk death to defend freedom in a military action, than to those who are sure they will die from hunger if they do not embrace a repressive regime that has its hands on the key to the pantry. We seem unable to understand why people will turn to an ideology that places first priority on the elemental ordering and sustaining of life rather than on freedom. We do this, not by some articulate analysis, but by refusing to take sufficient account of people's need for bread and then reacting in horror and dismay toward any groups that find something meaningful in a Marxist diagnosis of economic conditions, and a helping hand from the other side in the cold war conflict.

Nor dare we overlook the fact that in contrast to our professed love of freedom, our actions often send a message that the perpetuation in power of existing regimes which befriend us and support our policies, regardless of their record on freedom or human rights, is our uppermost objective. This policy estranges and discourages those movements in other countries that are justifiably yearning for freedom from harsh and vindictive conditions. We act with disdain, if not outright opposition, toward revolutionary movements that are more directed to the achievement of freedom than versed in the maintenance of order, or that believe it is possible to secure a just and sustaining distribution of bread only by the overthrow of unjust political and economic regimes. The result is that while we think of ourselves as the great defenders and advocates of freedom, we appear to many in the world as the great bulwark of the kind of order that is repressive and thwarts the hopes of those who would have a better life for themselves and their offspring. Often it is precisely our military posturing that gets us into this predicament, because the very nature of military thinking is to cherish order and to make alliances for its preservation without regard for other considerations.

If in a family one of the children reacts with hostility and hatred because it was denied acceptance and equality, we do not respond by cutting that child off from the family and condemning it with rhetoric and hatred. Instead, if we truly seek the well-being of both the child and the family, we show the child who feels cut off, knocked down, and deprived of the joys that family membership carries with it, an extra measure of concern and acceptance. Yet, often in our dealing with nations, or groups within nations, who have in exasperation resorted to revolution and violence in order to achieve greater justice, we respond with judgmental scolding. Some people become irate at any groups that befriend such movements, as have so many at the World Council of Churches because it has tried to befriend (not to aid and abet) groups combating racism in Africa and elsewhere.

If this irate condemnation of violence weren't so selective, it would be more persuasive. If our Government befriends nations that practice violations of civil rights—which violations often involve as much violence as does the behavior of liberation fighters—either we do not hear about it or we accept such an alliance with repression as the price of having allies in certain parts of the world. We thus get caught again, as inquisitors do so often, in acting as though it is legitimate to side with those who maintain order at the expense of freedom but not with those who seek freedom without sufficient regard for order.

If in a family unit one of the members tries to play other members against each other to escape responsibility by trying to get concessions first from one and then from another person in the household, we try to teach that member about the meaning of responsibility and the duty of membership in a group. Yet, in the larger relationships of life, such as exist between different nations, a number of big companies slide between the separate laws of individual nations to find havens from antipollution laws, escape from requirements that protect workers, or ways to reduce tax obligations. We seem to have neither the way —sometimes we do not even have the information that such behavior is going on—nor the will to elicit different behavior. There is nothing wrong with doing business in many different lands. Indeed, doing so may well help to cement contacts and create associations in many parts of the earth. It may develop our awareness beyond the confines of a single national perspective. However, if multinationals slide from country to country in a contrived policy to escape people-oriented regulations designed to further ordered justice in separate jurisdictions, they may fairly be accused of taking undue advantage of freedom and of eroding the welfare of the peoples affected by their activity. This can be the case even when no intended malice is involved and even when the presence of such groups within a country actually makes conditions there better than they might be without the groups' presence.

Undoubtedly most Americans believe that our nation—with its great heritage of a Declaration of Independence, with a Statue of Liberty (which has long been in disrepair) in its most famous harbor, and with the phrase "Life, Liberty and the pursuit of Happiness" in its heritage—stands as the foremost advocate of freedom in the contemporary world. Would that this were unexceptionally true. Many things, however, have entered into the record which prompt other peoples in the world to see us differently than we see ourselves. To understand why, we must look at the development of an international human rights movement and the relationship of U.S. policy to it.

In the late-nineteenth century, our country showed some interest in human rights and participated in the Brussels and Hague conventions, which redefined rules of war respecting the treatment of civilian noncombatants and prisoners of war. At the end of the First World War, President Woodrow Wilson proposed that we join a League of Nations, one purpose of which was to commit members to abide by a sense of human rights and to submit to a system of mandates for their enforcement. According to Article 22 of the Covenant for the League, if a member nation violated freedom of conscience and religion, went into slave trading, arms trading, or liquor traffic, its sovereignty could be invaded by the League to stop such a violation of the Covenant's provisions. Article 23 committed member nations also to refrain from permitting unfair or inhumane conditions of labor for men, women, and children, to limit trading in arms, to ensure freedom of speech, and to take positive action to eliminate disease. The Senate refused to ratify the treaty that would have placed the United States in the League of Nations, in part because President Wilson was so insistent it accept all the provisions.

Between 1789 and 1945 the United States entered into only one treaty relating to human rights. This was in 1926, when it signed a treaty providing for the suppression of slavery and banning trading in slaves. Our refusal to sign many proposed human rights treaties did not diminish our professed commitment to protect civil and political rights at home, but it did cast doubts about our willingness to support human rights elsewhere in the world.

At the outbreak of the Second World War, President Franklin D. Roosevelt sought to make our support for human rights more evident. In a speech to Congress on January 6, 1941, he made freedom from want, freedom from fear, freedom of expression, and freedom of religion key elements in a concept of human rights. He joined Winston Churchill in promulgating the Atlantic Charter in August of the same year, a document in which freedom from fear and freedom from want are two of eight key principles. Whether this was merely a means of developing the necessary ideological ground for entering the war or a genuinely idealistic proposal has been debated, but it did furnish a concrete historical act that identified America with a concern for human rights.

After the Second World War, the effort to establish the United Nations as a world organization to promote security and peace was accompanied by much concern for human rights. There was a movement to include in its charter an international bill of rights paralleling the Bill of Rights that found its way into the Constitution of the United States as an amendment. American religious leadership strongly backed such efforts, had a hand in helping to think about the draft, and in December of 1948 the General Assembly by a vote of 48 yeas and 8 abstentions approved a Universal Declaration of Human Rights. The United States was among those nations voting in favor. Some of those we now count as enemies and some we now treat as allies were in the group that abstained.

The text of the Universal Declaration of Human Rights deserves to be studied. It mentions as things to which persons are entitled, not only political freedom and equality under the law, but a right to social security, a right to work (including a right to the protection of a labor union in doing so), free choice of employment under just and favorable conditions, the right to an education, and other things significant for human well-being (such as food, clothing, housing, and medical care). The U.S.S.R. did not support the document, possibly because it called for more political freedom than her system allows. (Possibly the United States would have been more honest in rejecting it because it calls for more social welfare than our system provides.)

In 1954 the policy of the United States toward international human rights changed from active support, which involved treaty acceptance, to informal encouragement. This was, to a large extent, brought about by a shift from a concern for economic, social, and political betterment of places ravaged by war to a concern for the military defense of the nations in the anti-Communist bloc. Interwoven with this shift of posture was the controversy over the Bricker Amendment, which was aimed in part to protect individual states within our country from being bound to covenants or treaties made under United Nations auspices. A 1920 court case, *Missouri* v. *Holland* had held that treaty law takes precedence over conflicting laws within the political subjurisdictions of our country, and many people were concerned for a number of reasons about the effect of this upon the autonomy of the legislative process in the several states. Bricker's amendment would have prevented any treaty from abrogating a constitutionally protected right, from preventing any international organization from interfering with the domestic policies of the United States, and would have assured the success of these aims by requiring Congress to concur in all treaties to which the United States was a party by enacting them as legislation. Cynics like to observe that Bricker offered the amendment when the United States was considering a treaty with Canada that would have banned the duck hunting he liked to do on Lake Erie, but more serious questions were at stake.

President Dwight D. Eisenhower, through Secretary of State John Foster Dulles, sought to counteract the effect of such an amendment on the treaty-making functions of the executive branch of our Government. In order to head off the passage of the amendment, Dulles promised congressional leaders that the United States would no longer sign or become a party to UN human rights covenants. We would encourage their aims, but not commit ourselves to their provisions. This policy was first implemented in the refusal of the United States to sign the Convention on the Political Rights of Women. This change in U.S. policy left the many unaligned nations with the spectacle of both major powers refusing to be a party to anything more serious than rhetoric about human rights. It was this position that President Jimmy Carter sought to modify when he made a speech early in his presidency before the United Nations strongly backing the idea of human rights.

While President Carter gave much lip service to human rights, and signed and sent to the Senate for possible ratification at least three international conventions supporting them, many people have questioned how convincing our nation appears about this matter. We supported a regime in Iran that was noted for its use of repressive tactics against opposition; we have made wheat sales to the Soviets while watching underdeveloped nations experience great hunger; multinational corporations, perceived as mainly American, do business in lands with oppressive governments; and in our foreign policy we officially befriend some dictators whose support is strategically necessary to our cold war stance. These actions may make sense according to a war thinking that considers strategy as more crucial then credibility, but they are not the stuff of which peace is made.

THE GENERAL WELFARE AS A LARGER VISION

The difficulties that confront us in trying to think about the proper relationship between freedom and order can be resolved to a significant extent by employing another term that is central to our heritage. The Preamble to the Constitution of the United States, which contains the professed purposes for which it was written, lists these reasons for its drafting: "to form a more perfect Union, establish Justice, insure domestic Tranquility, provide for the common defence, promote the general Welfare, and secure the Blessings of Liberty to ourselves and our Posterity."

A careful scrutiny of this list will note that concerns about freedom, concerns about order, and concerns about well-being are equally emphasized. This is not a mere call for freedom. It is not a mere expression of the desire for order. Rather, it is a statement that highlights both freedom and order and sees them in relationship to a higher whole that our founding progenitors did not hesitate to call "the general welfare."

The term "welfare" has been so bandied into disrepute by an ideology of freedom in our recent domestic political scene that it may be dangerous to hold it up as meaningful —even if we do find it in the Preamble to the Constitution of the United States. But it points, as do few other terms, to a concept of social well-being that has enormous potential significance for thinking about peace. And it is closer in meaning to the biblical term for peace—*shalom*—than any other term in current usage. If a nation enjoys a general welfare, it is likely to be at peace. It will find ways to make freedom coexist with order and to make justice compatible with opportunity. Instead of repressive order it can cherish supportive community; instead of a freedom that is conjoined with inequity, it will cherish a liberty in which all are blessed. How did we ever fall into the reductionistic view that truncates our heritage into thinking that the only unquestioned function of government is to provide for the common defense?

In the Bible we find the well-being—the *shalom*—of the people given more attention than either freedom or order in themselves. The importance of freedom is never slighted; the importance of order is never denied. But neither of these is considered to be complete or to encompass the fullness of God's intentions for human destiny. Instead, the idea of justice is combined with the idea of steadfast love to create a sense of the human condition in which all fare well.

A land that fares well, and a globe that fares well, will be similar to other groups that fare well in their life together. A family that fares well knows the importance of both freedom and order and reconciles them in a harmonious experience of wholeness. Its members sense and share obligations and assume their orderly places in the scheme of things while they also enjoy freedom and cherish it for one another. A family that is fittingly knit and peacefully joined together does not see every extension of order as a denial of freedom or every exercise of freedom as a threat to order. Because it sees the overall welfare of all members as more important, it can provide both freedom and security to each of them.

If we are to be children of a God whose nature it is to work toward such an enriched and meaningful kind of human life, we shall have to be more serious about what welfare means, both for ourselves and for all the peoples of the earth.

IV

From Misunderstanding to Truth and from Suspicion to Trust

How we understand things largely determines how we deal with them. Distorted understandings of what is taking place in world events often lead to war and conflict. Distortions of reality pit group against group and raise suspicions about the motives, the intentions, and the integrity of others. We become both victims and purveyors of half-truths and untruths. Lies and deceptions are both the catalysts and the consequences of conflict. Only as truth prevails can peace be established. Alan Geyer is correct in asserting, "There is a largely unheralded connection between peace and truth which must be made firm if all the other themes in a theology of peace are to hold together."[13]

THE IMPORTANCE OF TRUTH

It has frequently been said that truth is the first casualty in wartime. When a nation engages in conflict it tends to put the best possible face on its cause, to claim victory regardless of how the fortunes of battle fare, and to be sure the people hear and come to believe the worst about the opponent. It tends to keep as secretive as possible about strategic plans, to throttle the flow of information so as to be able to surprise the enemy, and to discount the effects of endured casualties in order to keep good morale on the home front. Fighting seems to call for appearing tough rather than telling the truth, denying difficulties rather than admitting weaknesses, and drawing an absolute contrast between our virtue and the enemy's malice. Countries that normally protect and honor civil liberties, like freedom of speech and press, often suspend or limit them in times of war. Even if the free exchange of ideas is not officially curtailed, widespread hostility to unpopular views can put a crimping effect on public discourse in times of both hot wars and cold wars.

It is not always easy, particularly in times of conflict, to be sure what constitutes truth. Not only are there temptations to bottle up or misrepresent information that threatens a country's safety or lowers its morale, there are enormous difficulties in knowing what events mean. Truth involves having correct information, what people commonly call "facts," but knowledge of facts constitutes but a limited part of our understanding of reality. Indeed, as philosophy has pursued the quest for positive certainty about knowledge it has discovered that the things which can be known without a shred of doubt are very limited in number. If we are playing checkers, all the players can undoubtedly agree about how many pieces are left on the board. But let the board get spilled and the effort to replace things as they were will often evoke controversy. People don't remember things accurately. They are prone to think things are more favorable to themselves than to others. They may even try to take advantage of extenuating circumstances to advance their fortunes.

If the game involved is chess rather than checkers, the difficulties will be greater. If the game involved is life, and especially life between large conflicting groups, the difficulties are enormously compounded. It is not merely that more variables enter. People's perceptions of complex situations vary, not merely because their observations are inexact, but because their perception of events is colored by the circumstances in which they experience them. People's understandings of reality are formed by history and experience, by the social and cultural influences that have shaped and still shape their views, and by the underlying assumptions about reality that they use to interpret the data available to them. Some assumptions are freeing, others are enslaving. Some create and encourage harmony and community, but many are the very raw material of polarization and conflict.

In one of its more frequently quoted verses the Bible says, "You will know the truth, and the truth will make you free" (John 8:32). But religious ideas do not produce good consequences in any quick and easy manner. Think of how much harm has claimed the Bible as its inspiration, how much hostility and divisiveness have been generated by bombastically asserted positions claiming scriptural warrant. Many a cultured despiser of religion has asserted that if we could only rid the world of those "truths" asserted in the name of God, we would go a long way toward bringing peace to the world.

There are many in our culture who have tried to turn the biblical idea around, saying, if we are free, then we will surely discover the truth. Journalists, for example, often assume that if only the press is unfettered, truth will come forth. Academicians adhere to a code that gives priority to the absence of restraints and assumes that whatever is said or done under conditions of freedom will somehow be accurate and wise. Many skeptics and iconoclasts argue that if only we ignore traditions, abolish hierarchies, and do away with creeds, we will be well on the way to authentic truth. But freedom in and by itself no more guarantees truth than does an institutionalized or authoritarian definition.

Yet, we are to believe that truth is crucial to peace. We are to hope that peace and truth support each other, and that where one is the other will appear as well. A family is not likely to live in harmony until its members learn to share information with one another and to avoid downright lies and false innuendos that are useful for gaining privilege or advantage over one another. A family that learns as much as possible about the hopes and aspirations, the inadequacies and needs, even the shortcomings and vices of its members, can become peaceful and secure if it embraces that knowledge rightfully. It is not likely to be peaceful if its members do not know, or hide things from, one another.

We must attend, therefore, to the cultivation of our understanding. Fear and trembling rather than arrogance and certainty are the proper mood for doing this. We will undoubtedly find the world to be complex. We should be suspicious of simplistic analyses and glib suggestions. Instead of gravitating to explanations that give a single cause for events, we should look for more solid judgments. Instead of thinking that the lack of a spanking is all that has caused unruliness in siblings, we must realize how much love is required to raise good children. Instead of thinking that public crime has been caused only because we have not been harsh enough with unruly elements, we must realize how hard it is to create and protect civil order. Instead of thinking that life in the church would suddenly turn around if only one or two of the most troublesome members would be "called away"—whether to another city or to oblivion we do not specify—we must realize how difficult it is to create a true community of faith. Instead of thinking that the world would be a wholly different place if only one country, whose policies we think are responsible for many of the problems, would bite the dust of atomic cloud, or be so fearful of having to do so as to behave in a wholly new manner, we must realize how complex are the problems of the world. As long as our assumptions continually conjure up enemies in our minds and lead us to believe that the problems we face will be resolved merely by seeing them put down, our policies will undoubtedly be based on a simplistic polarizing model that largely rules out the making of peace.

But if we can be misled by thinking too simplistically, we can also be misled by thinking too cynically. If we are prone to a calculative prudence and a disposition to doubt that anything is realistic unless it posits the worst of possibilities, then we will gravitate toward understandings that stifle hope. In doing this we are not being governed by some objective set of facts that warrant pessimism, but by a covert world view that takes all data to be a confirmation of its worst expectations. It is no more "realistic" always to believe the worst about every situation than it is to believe that there is a possibility of something good emerging from it. The hard-nosed skeptic, who always sees the thorns rather than the blooms on the rosebush, is not necessarily more accurate in grasping what is real than the person who entertains hope and posits the possibility of surprise. The person who sees in international events—and particularly in the behavior of those we deem our enemies—only the possibility of conflict and the inevitability of trouble is not necessarily any more aware of the truth than the person who can see the possibility of reconciliation.

Our understandings are colored by assumptions used to formulate them. We can, to adopt a much-used figure of speech, call these underlying assumptions "myths." The term is much used in theological discourse to indicate a governing way of considering evidence that is not articulated in propositional terms. Our myths determine how we look at historical, social, and political events and arrive at a judgment as to their meaning. Myths in this sense function in every kind of complex understanding.

They shape our perceptions of life and influence our judgments about the possibilities within it. Some thinkers call
these overarching outlooks "paradigms"—a term somewhat more attractive to modern ears.

Whatever we call these controlling frameworks within
which we think, we should realize they are very central in
the process of understanding. They may dominate our
judgment so completely as to make it impossible for us to
see things that do not fit the interpretative scheme which
we use. Of course, when the data do not coincide with the
controlling myth or paradigm, our way of understanding
things has to be reconsidered. But the marvel is how massive must be the incongruity and dissonance before a myth
gets overthrown. Life in the world is so complex, so laced
with ambiguity, so replete with mixed signals, and so burdened with the sin of both ourselves and others, that we
change our way of looking at the world only in the rarest
circumstances. Usually, we filter all evidence through a
dispositional screen that remains fairly constant.

Generally, those who look at life with a tendency to see
its darker side are called "realists" while those who tend
to see its brighter side are "idealists." Curiously, realists
seem to ignore contrary evidence more readily than do
idealists. One good action on the part of a nation considered to be an enemy doesn't force the realist to do a
convictional flip and suddenly think things have taken a
different course, but one contradictory indication often
throws an idealist into a tailspin. As long as we allow negative dissonance to destroy positive understandings of reality more readily than we allow positive dissonance to over-
ride negative understandings of reality, we shall live in a
world of people who believe the worst about what may
happen instead of working, where possible, for something
better.

Sources of Liberating Insight

The frameworks that shape our understanding are more like gifts than private creations. They are formed by the experiences we have, and particularly the experiences we have in the company of others. Our myths or paradigms are formed very largely by the neighborhoods that give us roots, the vocational settings in which we earn our livelihoods, the social circuits in which we recreate, and the political units of which we are citizens. It is very important from whom such signals come. Totalitarianisms try to collapse all influences into a single monolith controlled by the state and by an official ideology, thus obtaining mastery of the dominant myth. This indicates how well they understand the social sources of knowing. More pluralistic and open societies do not, and cannot, monitor the influences so tightly, but they too can be affected by strongly controlling outlooks.

The country in which people live provides one of the most powerful frameworks for their interpretation of, and response to, events. Even in a free society the political framework is very crucial. It may be present so pervasively that we do not realize how much it dominates our thinking. We can be shocked into realizing how strongly myths operate by hearing views that were taken as almost self-evident in some past period, but that now seem quaint to us. For instance, consider the controlling assumptions of many people at the turn of the century, as revealed in this speech by the junior senator from Indiana.

> We will not renounce our part in the mission of the race, trustee, under God, of the civilization of the world. . . . He has made us . . . the master organizers of the world to establish system where chaos reigns. . . . He has made us adept in government that we may

administer government among savage and senile
peoples. . . . And of all our race, He has marked the
American people as His chosen Nation to finally lead
in the regeneration of the world. This is the divine
mission of America, and it holds for us all the profit,
all the glory, all the happiness possible to man. We
are trustees of the world's progress, guardians of its
righteous peace. The judgment of the Master is upon
us: "Ye have been faithful over a few things; I will
make you ruler over many things."[14]

Patriotic groupthink, which lies back of such a blatant
statement of manifest destiny, may not be nearly so powerful now as it was even as recently as a generation ago.
However, it is still powerful. It may arise because most
schooling has loyalty to the civil order as its highest commitment. It may arise because the political process depends upon the imagery and ritual of patriotism more
than upon prophetic correctives. It may arise because the
communications and media sector that shapes public opinion—while often critical and even withering in its com-
mentary on public officials—has no significant vision of life
other than that of the culture to which it belongs, and
often little more than the popularity figures of the ratings
to measure its effectiveness.

We cannot disconnect from the political order to which
we belong. But we can make allowances for how it shapes
our thinking so that we do not make a gospel-like truth out
of the gossip-like input that comes to us from the sur-
rounding climate of opinion. Moreover, we can search for
contacts that enable us to transcend the geographical, economic, and political stratifications into which we are often
isolated.

One of the communities that can transcend national
identity is the church. Both individual communions and
the ecumenical movement provide broader experiences
than those which are possible on a local or merely national

basis. The Anglican Communion, for example—not least because of years of missionary work—has more members in Africa than it does in all the rest of the world combined. Presbyterianism is strong in Southeast Asia; Roman Catholicism, in South and Central America. Christian groups hold on with heroic vitality in situations of persecution and oppression, often hoping very much to be understood in their efforts to comprehend the meaning of the gospel in political/economic circumstances that differ from those in the Western world. One of the striking developments of the last thirty years has been the creation of a strong and extensive network of different church bodies from every part of the world that have met together and talked to each other, sometimes confrontationally, about fundamental issues facing the human race in these times. The leadership of the World Council of Churches, which is the body most representative of this development, has shifted away from Anglo-Saxon males to a diverse group of persons drawn from many nations.

What an opportunity this provides to learn more fully the hopes, the aspirations, the perspectives—and just as importantly, the fears and resentments—that are harbored by a large number of people from all places on the globe. Those who work in the global ministries of the several denominations come up against these attitudes all the time.

It is not always comforting to have assumptions challenged or horizons broadened. At the 1979 meeting of the Conference on Faith, Science, and the Future, sponsored by the World Council of Churches in Cambridge, Massachusetts, Americans were sometimes shocked by what they heard. Third World delegates often forcefully declared that science and technology curse rather than bless the lives of people where they live. Even the arrangements of the conference were such that many Americans found themselves unable to obtain delegate status because there were so many others from different nations who wanted to attend. Those who were given observer rather than delegate status had to live in satellite accommodations across the river. For those who attended, this was a learning experience that forced a reexamination of many assumptions. When encounters like this take place in an organization like the United Nations it may be possible to dismiss the polarizations as largely political, but when they take place between persons professing the same loyalty to Jesus Christ, it is not so easy to discount them without repudiating the unity of those who believe the gospel.

Unfortunately, for many professing members of churches, religious faith has to do only with private living or with the concerns of the local parish. Many churches, by polity or by disposition, have little interest in, knowledge about, or contact with ecumenical activities. What they do hear may prompt them to resent and resist the challenges that are bound to come from such experiences. Since the fastest growing part of the church is found in other parts of the globe, it follows that the weight of ecumenical activities will increasingly shift to other lands, not all of whose people have the same political system or economic attitudes as Americans. Many Americans are disconcerted when they have to justify their political and social way of thinking in conversations with those of quite different persuasions. Frequently they demand that their churches or denominations get out of ecumenical involvements. This only further cuts them off from a very valuable source of information that can help to enlarge their way of seeing the world. Meanwhile, the secular press and the broadcast media either completely ignore, or even report unsympathetically on, the momentous developments in a truly worldwide Christian movement whose various members interpret the will of God from many perspectives.

Fortunately, it is possible for horizons of understanding

to be broadened by experiences in local parishes. Attitudes do get turned around by unexpected events. Some years ago, one church, like so many others in America, was deeply skeptical of the Nestlé boycott. This was begun some years ago when The Nestlé Company persisted in marketing infant formula in lands where impure water makes its use dangerous. Then two doctors, each respected in both the church and in the community it serves, took temporary mission assignments in Africa. Upon their return, those doctors were able to explain the havoc wrought by bottle feeding in lands where the water is usually impure, and their firsthand account of the problem did much to change the attitude of that congregation. Nothing in the public clamor about the rights of companies to put out products and to advertise their use could match the quiet power of Christian witness arising from firsthand experience and authenticated by a record of sacrificial service.

Another church gets actively involved in the Heifer Project, which sends different kinds of livestock to lands that are battling against hunger and starvation. But this church is not content merely to provide money for this purpose. It sees that representatives of the congregation visit the place where that animal it has sponsored has been sent. This supplements their material help with personal contact. When those who have gone as envoys of the congregation return they have much to share that enlarges horizons and changes viewpoints. World Communion in that church is a transformed and transforming celebration.

It is, of course, a risk/venture to believe that the truth which helps to overcome divisive hostility between the peoples of the world can be grasped quickly enough, or on a sufficiently broad scale, to counteract the ignorance and distrust that surrounds us. But such a risk/venture is at the center of what it means to believe that the truth will make us free. Unless we are open to the work of truth, our lives will lack vision and understanding. "Where there is no vision, the people perish." (Prov. 29:18.)

THE IMPORTANCE OF TRUST

Not only does the way we think about others greatly affect our behavior toward them, but the way others think about us greatly determines their behavior toward us. Hence we must consider not only how our search for truth is related to the making of peace but how to make ourselves trustworthy in the eyes of others.

There are many ways to lack credibility in the international scene, and the United States has unwittingly fallen into a number of them. Its problems may begin with its history, which is replete with the use of violence. This nation acquired the geographical space in which it lives by forcefully ousting a people here before it. It then developed and maintained a slavery system unparalleled for its commerce in human lives and lasting far later than did slavery in most other civilized countries. It was able to throw off that slavery system only by violence. America is the only nation in the world that has ever used atomic weapons, and it did so by destroying the entire population of two cities. Most recently, American military power was employed against the people of Vietnam in a horrendous campaign of counterinsurgency with technologically advanced weapons that wreaked havoc on both the countryside and the people of a nation halfway around the globe. This history has to be counterweighed before we are likely to persuade the world that the prospects of peace rest entirely with us.

Moreover, many features of American life leave others wondering about our intentions. While our political process is remarkably stable, the policies that come from it are not. The bipartisan foreign policy that developed after the

Second World War produced a long period of support for such programs as the Marshall Plan and Point Four and encouraged our participation in organizations like the United Nations. This bipartisan foreign policy has now given way to two sharply different approaches to dealing with our responsibilities in the world. These views do not distinguish the major political parties from each other as much as different segments within each of the parties. This makes it difficult to effect a policy choice between them.

The new polarization is between an approach that is global in concern and understands the task to be one of considering the interests of many nations on their own terms and one that posits a simple confrontation between two giant powers to which everything else is seen as secondary. This new polarization is between an approach that regards the United Nations (with all of its problems) as an important forum for airing of grievances and lowering of tensions and one that is openly critical and almost contemptuous of that body because it has great difficulty being decisive about particular issues. This new polarization is between a view that it is important and possible to pursue the reduction of armaments by careful agreement to ensure that all nations do so together and a view that only the exercise of power counts and that armaments must be stockpiled in ever-escalating proportions. This polarization is between a view that diplomacy can be imaginatively used to achieve a less polarized world and one that sees value primarily in military arrangements that preserve present alignments of power.

The leadership of our nation changes quite frequently, and with the changes come differences in leadership style. During one quadrennium we have a President who talks much about human rights and during the next we have a President who speaks more about the need to be strong and powerful. Sometimes the rhetoric of the leaders changes more than the official policy of the nation. America has been involved in talks about disarmament under both kinds of president; it has engaged in programs of aid and mutual assistance under both kinds of president. It has restrained from pulling the genie of chaos from the bottle of atomic destruction under both kinds of president.

Those who look at our nation from outside sometimes wonder how our professions correspond to our actions. It would serve us well as a people to have a more enduring understanding of the nature of peace and our role among the nations so that excessive rhetoric would not seem to be so useful in political campaigning and the signals sent out by it not be so confusing.

There has probably been no greater cause for the distrust with which our nation is viewed from many quarters in the world than the development, since the late 1940s, of a new kind of intelligence operation. Spying is one thing and it has a traditional place in affairs between nations. It is an old "honorable game." But the use of covert strategies to interfere in the affairs of other nations is something else. Yet, our Central Intelligence Agency has regularly gone beyond spying and used stealth and intrigue to alter military and political situations in many parts of the world.

It is hard to make a judgment as to whether these covert operations have made any difference in the power factors that effect our national security. The data by which to judge that are by the very nature of the process unavailable for public analysis. But it is not hard to show that the very process of setting up an agency in our Government to engage in unacknowledged acts of violence around the world has had an adverse effect upon America's image. We have paid a high price for an unknown gain.

Totalitarian regimes do not need to account for their actions to their people or to be honest with the world. We criticize them because of this. A democracy, in contrast, that engages in undercover and unacknowledged operations contradicts the very premises upon which it is founded as a nation. When it acts like the nations it so frequently criticizes it gives up one of the most valuable qualities it possesses for achieving credibility among the nations.

Perhaps no development in America's recent history shows more clearly how the pressure of the cold war has caused us to anesthetize our moral sensitivities. The apostasy involved is demonstrated ironically by an inscription on the south wall of the central lobby of the CIA's headquarters, where John 8:32 is inscribed: "You shall know the truth, and the truth shall make you free." Perhaps the information gathered by spying might be useful in preserving national security. But clandestine actions taken against others can have no such meaning. They belong to a realm of distrust in which power is believed to be the only operative reality, and force the only way to exercise it. The covert actions of our intelligence agency have undercut the credibility of the diplomatic process, and have created a situation in which America can be blamed for anything unsavory that goes on in other lands. Although it might take a long time for others to believe we had made it, nothing less is needed than a clean, public break with this sort of national behavior.

Finally, our credibility in the world has been eroded because many multinational corporations, which are identified as being American, have done business overseas without being concerned for the ways in which their presence relates to local aspirations for political and social freedom. Certainly it is difficult to make the reform of a repressive regime a precondition for doing business with, or under, it. Sometimes the presence of external economic power has benefits for people who live under repressive governments. America often gets identified with regimes with which multinationals do business and comes to be blamed for contributing to repression. The result is not

intentional. Many who do business overseas are as dedicated as any of us to a belief in the importance of freedom
as an ideal. But as long as the bottom line for doing things
commercially overseas is economic return alone, this
problem will not go away.

During the First World War we said that we were entering the conflict in Europe to make the world safe for democracy. We learned that such an outcome was no easy
one to obtain, and that what may be won in battles on the
military front is not always brought into political reality.
Indeed, right now there are many people in many parts of
the world wondering which of the major powers shows by
its action and behavior where the cause of human well-
being lies. Some are actually wondering whether or not
democracy is safe for the world. We must become concerned to show that it is. To do so we must indicate that
violence need not be a prevalent feature of a free society,
that elections do not need to depend upon bombastic rhetoric, that unacknowledged interference with the affairs of
other nations under the cover of intelligence is really quite
unintelligent, and that our economic system need not necessarily thwart the aspiration of people for greater justice
in their countries. Only to the extent that we can do this
will we engender the trust upon which peace can be built.

V

From Hostility to Composure and Compassion

From time to time some event reveals how fragile is the civility that keeps life from slipping into a violent brawl. It may be a little incident. If a waiting car stalls as a traffic light turns from red to green at a busy intersection, its driver will undoubtedly feel embarrassed about blocking traffic. The other drivers, even if they can get around the stalled vehicle, will often react with much contempt. Honking horns and withering stares reveal an underlying hostility, which swells to the surface like molten lava from a subterranean caldron. Some years ago, following a change in the rule for issuing transfers on New York City's transportation lines, a passenger in Brooklyn shot a bus driver who would not follow the old procedure of issuing a free coupon. Hostility is not only close to the surface, but can be uncommonly extreme.

THE ANATOMY OF HOSTILITY

It may be a far cry from impatience at a traffic light or the shooting of a bus driver to contemplating the possible annihilation of other nations, but while the scale of the encounter changes and the actors differ, all these events involve an anatomy of hostility upon which conflict thrives. War depends upon the hostility that people feel toward others with sufficient intensity to wish their inconvenience, to seek their downfall, or even to plan their destruction. We must recognize hostility as a pervasive and deep malady in our midst that has to be overcome if we are to move to the creation of a peaceful community.

The simplest manifestations of hostility are agitation and truculence. Agitation involves emotionally distraught responses to complexity and change. Those who cannot cope with the difficult process of interacting with others or with the ordinary stresses that all living involves become agitated. Weak and insecure people are often agitated. Domestic violence is most common where the partners are inadequate to the stresses of life, insecure with themselves and with each other, and where they feel incapable of meeting the demands imposed upon them by a joint relationship. Curiously, agitated people often bristle truculently. Truculence is a self-assertive attempt to command situations, even ferociously. The more that agitated people become truculent, the more they are apt to cause others to react to them with a distrust that aggravates their feelings of inadequacy. The process may feed upon itself, causing first a spiral and then a whirling vortex that results in some irrational or violent response.

Hostility also appears as anger and frenzy. Some anger is legitimate and healthy, but anger that is mixed with hostility becomes an intense and compulsive condition that eclipses or destroys the deliberate and intentional control of the emotions that is necessary for a humane quality of life. Frenzy turns upon others with a furious antagonism. Frenzied individuals are at war, perhaps with themselves and certainly with others. Frenzied anger thrives on rage and seeks to destroy the object of its hostility. It showers hatred on those who differ while madly supporting and uncritically embracing those in whom it finds allies. The effects of frenzy often last far longer than the reasons that first brought it into being.

Contempt is another form of hostility. Contempt arises when differences between people become occasions of bad feelings. People can despise both those whom they consider inferior, in which case contempt takes the form of disdain, and those whom they consider superior, in which case contempt takes the form of envy. Contempt often takes the form of scapegoating. In scapegoating, others get blamed for ills and difficulties far beyond their control or influence. When contempt is present, social differentiations become the basis for pecking orders that corrupt those who create them and embitter those whom they victimize. The effect on good feelings between persons is devastating. Contempt is closely related to conflict because the elixir of self-concern on which it breeds brews a poison of bitterness and rancor.

To avoid contempt does require us to ignore evidence. In contrast to those who hate ideologically, the victims of wrongs often describe their plight without rhetorical overkill. For example, atrocity stories that recount a tragic firsthand experience are often more carefully nuanced and stated with a fundamental objectivity that is lacking when tragedy stories are used melodramatically to whip up hostility. Like the righteous anger of the prophet who conducts a lover's quarrel with a covenanted group, the carefully stated complaints by victims of oppression are primarily directed at the alleviation of an evil rather than at the inculcation of contempt.

Communication is difficult when hostility is present. Communication involves an exchange of ideas and information, and also a sharing of feelings and hopes. If people have different views of the world and sharply different value systems, then the exchange of information is more difficult and the interfacing of ideas for common purposes almost impossible. Think, for instance, how much more difficult even dinner conversation is if the guests are members of different political parties or are strongly committed to different religious views.

It is even more difficult to communicate across the boundaries of nations having deep social and political differences. Bombast, epithet, innuendo, ridicule, and caricature become the stock-in-trade of much political and international oratory. When hostility dominates, rhetoric turns into an instrument of conflict. Intergroup communication is poisoned and inflamed. Polarizing rhetoric, which appears regularly under conditions of hostility, fulfills the twin functions of trumpeting one's own virtues and tearing down those of an opponent. The result is the antithesis of communication. We sometimes call it propaganda, but the term is too weak. It is nothing less than a betrayal of what communication ought to be.

The objective assessment of dangers in which circumstances are judiciously weighed is one thing; polarizing rhetoric, another. George Kennan has examined changes that have taken place in Soviet-American relationships. Kennan is no sentimentalist about the Soviet Union, yet he has been appalled by the mood swings that characterize the American attitude. Decrying both the tendency to overlook the problems posed by Communism when Russia was on the side of the allies in the Second World War, and the complete reversal that has been operative in the cold war period, he indicates how false and unrealistic it is to picture Russia as "a monster devoid of all humanity and of all rationality of motive, at once the embodiment and the caricature of evil, devoid of internal conflicts and problems of its own, intent only on bringing senseless destruction to the lives and hopes of others."[15] Yet does not such a mind-set lie behind the unmitigated assertion that the Soviet system constitutes "the focus of evil in the modern world"[16]?

It serves emotional needs to whip up a feeling that an

enemy is not fit to belong in the human family. It serves emotional needs to contend that only our side is moral or worthy. Polarizing rhetoric permits no careful nuancing of pros and cons. It must picture adversaries as totally evil, friends as altogether righteous. Even compatriots who will not join in such a chorus of absolutizing distinctions come to be treated as heretical or subversive. The process of putting others down becomes very heady.

Hostility creates the psychic possibility of conflict. It takes differences that might be tolerable under ordinary circumstances, and that might be resolved by negotiation, and turns them into absolute stands that can only collide. It overrides all considerations that would preserve balance in the appraisal of the relative merits of two contending parties. Hostility often invokes the sanction of religion to make ordinary differences into total distinctions, and those who differ into devil figures. This robs the antagonist of moral standing. No antagonism is too strong, no action too destructive, no hatred too great, if it is aimed against those who come thus to be pictured as the enemies of God.

COMPOSURE AS A STEP TOWARD PEACE

How can we move away from hostility, away from the agitation and the polarization that lead to conflict? What concepts point to an alternative way of thinking, to a way of thinking that can counteract the destructive consequences of interpersonal enmity and intergroup hatred?

An initial step in this process can be made by looking at a little-used word that can point to a much-needed quality in human behavior. Many other words help point to the same idea, but some of them are already burdened with distracting implications. We can speak of moderation, of poise, of calmness, of serenity, of gentleness, of graciousness, and of sobriety. Each of these terms points to an attitude of mind and heart that can counteract hostility.

The word "composure" may help even more. Those who
would make peace must be composed, that is, they must
deal with life and with others so as to build up rather than
to tear down goodwill.

The starting experience of being composed is to know
ourselves as the object of God's caring love. "If God is for
us," asked Paul from the midst of troubles and persecu-
tions that tried his spirit, "who is against us?" (Rom. 8:31).
Paul showed that it is precisely because God justifies and
intercedes for us that "we are more than conquerors
through him who loved us" (v.37). We are composed, that
is, we are "put together," by a power of wholeness that
transforms our being without overpowering our surroundings or necessarily destroying our antagonists. As we are
renewed by grace we are enabled to do what is good. We
are enabled to love because we are first loved, and because
the appropriate response to being loved by God is to show
forth love to others.

Becoming composed is not an experience of being rendered weak or of behaving supinely before others. It does
not consist of a bucolic state that is concerned only for
individual comfort and escape from issues or problems.
Composed persons master situations primarily by not
being flustered by them. Whereas the insecure grow increasingly agitated as events become more difficult to deal
with, persons of inward composure become more and
more poised as conditions get troubling.

All the dimensions of hostility are divisive. They frag-
ment and destroy. They "decompose" situations. If we are
to make peace, we shall have to learn a different art—both
as individuals and as nations. We shall have to counteract
vindictive hatred. Whereas self-righteous fury breeds contempt, composure helps us to feel important without having to make others feel unimportant. Whereas hostility
depends on polarizing rhetoric, composure repudiates the
diatribe as unworthy of those who know themselves loved

and redeemed by God. Composure would bring as many as possible into a great composite rather than fragmenting differing groups into armed camps dedicated only to the protection or perpetuation of their own righteousness.

Composure will also lead to more adequate communication. True communication starts to be possible when each party to an argument first learns to state the position of the other party with such care as to prompt the other party to acknowledge the correctness of the description. This test, applied to both personal and political utterances, would go a long way to reinstate communication in situations that have come to be marked only by polarizing rhetoric. Observing this rule would get us beyond the callous putdown, the unfair gibe, the thoughtless epithet. It might even enable us to discover that, while others see the world quite differently than we do, their perspective makes a kind of sense. Further, such care in the exploration of issues might, in turn, enable others to realize why we think as we do. It may be naive to hope for this kind of communication. Few exchanges between contending factions in the world today give us reason for thinking that the skills required to achieve it are commonly available. If we are to avoid using bombs, we would do well to avoid using *bomb*ast.

Communication helps to overcome antagonisms in proportion to the degree that it deals directly with basic points at issue and openly canvasses fundamental differences. To abandon affirmations or to adopt a noncommittal pluralism that treats all points of view as equally legitimate simply because they are espoused with equal sincerity does not help communication. We may have to do this about certain matters to keep "truces" in polite society, but where communication is abandoned for the sake of casual harmony, something vitally essential to rich human relationships is lost. The ability to canvass issues until each side fully knows the position of the other and the key matters of disagreement, and then respects the integrity with which that position is held, provides the only possibility for putting things together. Those who pick their associations so as always to be talking to people whose views are congenial cannot learn to communicate in ways that will heal the world. It is more heroic to wrestle with the problems of a contentious group than to smother in the congeniality of a friendly one.

As we think about communication, it is sobering to reflect upon the state of language learning in our country. In most nations of comparable professed achievement people learn at least one other language as a matter of course. Not so in the United States. Americans expect others to know English but do not generally master another living tongue. The contrast between the number of Russians who learn to speak English and the few and dwindling number of Americans who master Russian reveals our implicit disinterest in communication. The same is true in relation to our Spanish-speaking neighbors to the south. We expect others to communicate with us only on our linguistic terrain. Meanwhile, when educational deficiencies become public laments, it is mathematics and science that lend themselves to warmaking that are usually stressed, not the language skills that might help in peacemaking.

Nor is composure to be confused with an indifference induced by numbing the emotions. The cure for antagonistic feelings is not a denial of the emotions, but a deep involvement in seeing that things come together. People whose faculties are impaired by drugs, by alcoholic excess, by the overstimulation of a scramble for privilege, or by inordinate infatuation with spectator conflict, are not composed. They have deadened rather than mastered their feelings. They have learned to be callous toward injustice and to neglect offenses done to others. This anesthetized opaqueness to the crying need of a bruised world has become such a widespread way of life as to put a question mark beside every prospect for well-being in these times. Rome had circuses to keep its population inured to brutality and injustice. America has electronic devices and other diversions.

Nothing in the foregoing analysis posits a sharply etched distinction between composed behavior in individuals or in small groups and composed behavior in larger groups or in the relationships between great powers. A nation will do well, just as an individual does well, to avoid the frenzied anger that prevents it from recognizing when a situation calling for wariness and caution has turned into a situation in which trust is possible. A nation does well, just as an individual does well, to avoid scapegoating and to avoid the rhetoric of hostility. A nation does well, just as an individual does well, to keep open every possibility for communication by seeking to understand adequately and represent fairly the positions of those with whom it has to coexist. A nation does well, just as an individual does well, to profess its convictions as a means of identifying itself rather than as a means of trumpeting its superiority. A nation does well, just as an individual does well, to avoid the stupors of insensitivity or the luxury of interacting only with friends.

There is no necessary reason why humility, reserved poise, and dialogical openness cannot have corporate as well as individual expressions. There is no reason why politicians, to gain influence at home, have to utilize inflaming rhetoric against peoples outside. There is no reason why toughness needs to be the only coin of the political realm, or why polarizing debate has to be the only kind that brings forth response. There is no reason why being tough-minded has to entail being hostile. There is no reason why siding with allies needs to involve blindness to their shortcomings, or why guarding flanks against potential adversaries demands an unconditional condemnation of everything they do. There is no reason why the further cementing of friendly ties that already exist has completely to negate efforts to create friendly ties where they do not yet exist. The question that Jesus put to his disciples, "If you salute only those who love you, what more are you doing than others?" (Matt. 5:47) can be legitimately put to nations as well as to individuals.

Composure, which comes from the same root as the word "composition," implies a "putting together" of things into meaningful, artistic, and productive wholes that can be enjoyed and celebrated. It stands against that frame of mind which divides, misconstrues, and separates life into warring camps and belligerent units.

INDIVIDUAL AND POLITICAL COMPASSION

Composure depends for its fullest cultivation upon another quality that marks human life at its best. This quality, which is known as compassion, acknowledges our closeness to our neighbors and prompts us to share in their feelings and yearnings. We are compassionate when, as did the good Samaritan, we care for those who have suffered misfortune. But the meaning of the term can include not only the alleviation of misfortune but the counteracting of hostility.

The initial movement in exercising compassion is to become aware of another's need. Many people do not take sufficient account of this first element in compassion. While they would probably not refuse to perform an act of charity if confronted with a crying need, neither do they go around seeking to locate distress to alleviate. While they would not, at least by profession, pass by a traveler in trouble on the highway (though it happens all the time on the superhighways), neither would they go about looking for people to whom to minister. While quite willing to respond to cries of distress they hear, most people do not feel compelled to search out the weary, the hurt, the needy, or the bruised.

It may be that the most prevalent shortcoming in the exercise of compassion lies not in a malicious callousness that deliberately refuses to alleviate perceived distress but in a widespread tendency so to position ourselves as never to see any distress. Who can be expected to respond to needs that are so far away that we might learn about them only by the most extraordinary probing? To take compassion seriously is to be attuned to all the needs that might be learned about and not merely the ones that scream to us from the immediate range of attention. This imposes an overwhelming, almost impossible, obligation that exceeds rational prudence.

An obligation that seemingly knows no limits is much akin to the obligation Christ portrayed with the various contrasts he made between the old law and the new law in the Sermon on the Mount. Instead of avoiding overt murder, Christ indicates we are to avoid even anger (Matt. 5:21–26); instead of avoiding an act of infidelity, we are to avoid even the thought of doing so (vs. 27–30); instead of avoiding only unfair divorce, we are to avoid divorce altogether (vs. 31–32); instead of uttering the truth only when under oath (or, dare we add, when wired up to a lie detector?), we are to be truthful all the time (vs. 33–37); instead of dealing with others only within the strict bounds of reciprocity, we are to go twice as far as tormentors require (vs. 38–42); instead of loving only those who love us, we are expected also to love enemies (vs. 43–48). We can therefore suggest, without doing violence to this way of thinking: instead of showing care only for our nearest associates, we are to open ourselves to all who are in need.

Clearly, we are not likely to show compassion to all others in the world if we have separated the world into groups we consider deserving of care and those we consider not. Hence, reconciliation must be the partner of compassion. We can only be as compassionate as love requires if we overcome the divisions that persist in our political lives. While it is impossible to show mercy to others until we have come to know them, it can be hypocritical to show it to those whom we continue to distrust or hate. "First be reconciled . . ." comes the biblical admonition. Only reconciliation makes compassion possible without bad faith.

To be reconciled to the world involves nothing less than a conversion. This conversion would involve our whole being—our way of thinking, of feeling, and of responding. Too often Christians have popularized a thinking about conversion that amounts to little more than a call to change opinions about certain propositions. Even that kind of Christianity, in many instances, has made helpful transformations in people's lives. But to make conversion only a matter of changing belief systems, and rebirth only a private experience, is to relegate the significance of the gospel to changes in individuals. It is no wonder that the idea of conversion is looked upon with suspicion by many people who know in their inner hearts that something more corporate is needed. We need a conversion that changes the whole being, and the whole being—not merely of individuals but of social groups and the life of nations. Though the difficulties of having such a turning around are staggering, we must not conclude they are insurmountable. To do that would be to limit the significance of God's saving work to private individuals alone and to confine the corporate structures of the world to inevitable disaster. There is little biblical warrant for this splitting apart of the realm of redemption.

The dictionary definition and common usage seem to confine thinking about compassion to instances that involve the alleviation of distress and suffering. But the construction of the word itself (which combines a root that means together with a stem that means to feel) warrants attention to a sharing of joys as well as distresses. Henri J. M. Nouwen writes: "Compassion also means sharing another's joy which can be just as difficult as suffering with him. To give another the chance to be completely happy and to let his joy blossom to the full [can also be a part of compassion]."[17]

To share joys and accomplishments with others needs to be as much an aspect of our faith endeavors as to alleviate distresses. If, either as individuals or as groups, we keep others at a distance from us, so that there is no entry into each other's experiences, no walking together in duty or in joy, no relationships built up under creative and constructive circumstances, then the chance of showing compassion to them in times of trouble becomes all but precluded. If hostility does not stand in the way, we should find it possible to share joys in accomplishments even across political differences. We need not approve all that another nation does to take note of the things in its life that we can admire, like the fact Russia has raised her literacy rate nearly ninefold. Why can't cultural exchanges allow joys to be shared with countries whose political systems we do not approve? Why can't we be compassionate toward others if they manage to alleviate human need in their midst? If our stance is such that we can make no move to find common grounds for celebration of significant achievements, then indeed the possibility of being compassionate will be cut off at the very roots.

A reconciling and compassionate response to others will change experience radically. It will, in the first place, transform the function and significance of power. Without compassion and in the absence of reconciliation, power becomes an instrument of rancor and division. Through power we can lord it over others, and frighten those whom we do not like or whom we fear so that they will not try to lord it over, or be able to frighten us. Such power depends upon a massive capacity to inflict adversity upon known, imagined, or hypothetical enemies. It is a means of "putting down" or "fending off" others. This is just as operative in the case of individuals who cannot love as it is in the case of nations that cannot live in peace. In his book *Power and Innocence,* Rollo May explains what happens when individuals are reconciled. They are enabled to build relationships with others by an empowerment that comes from love. Rejecting the sharp dichotomy between loveless power and powerless love, May suggests how a different conception of power is compatible with an experience of love. "Love needs power," he writes, "if it is to be more than sentimentality and . . . power needs love if it is not to slide into manipulation."[18]

Can large group relationships undergo the transformation that Rollo May indicates is possible in the case of individuals? Clearly some have. Germany and France are no longer harsh rivals; India and Great Britain consider themselves friends; Egypt and Israel have transformed their relationship to each other. International enmities are transformed by much the same dynamic as personal enmities are relieved. Think, for instance, of the contrasting tone between the making of our peace with Germany at the end of the First and at the end of the Second World Wars. In the first instance the primary mood of the victors was to humiliate and punish the wrongdoing of the vanquished. But that only embittered a highly cultured nation, and in part sowed the seeds of resentment which (along with other factors) made things ripe for Hitler's rise to power. The mood at the conclusion of the Second World War was different. Perhaps we were only calculating how to create a strong West Germany and a viable Japan to take their place in the power equation of a cold war. But we did act so as to empower both former enemies to become partners. It is less likely now that a demagogue will arise in either country today than was the case because of the internal conditions that were created after the vindictive settlement of the First World War.

Vindictiveness is bad therapy for wrongdoing. Revenge leaves human feelings woefully distorted and out of kilter. It invites backlash and pours poisons into the sores of defeat. It creates a vicious circle that becomes more difficult to break with every cycle. Blood feuds between small family groups illustrate these dynamics just as vividly as do the cycles of conflict, victory, vindictiveness, and war that go on between nations. Any punishment that is meted out apart from compassion, and without being accompanied by loving support that makes those involved aware that they are desired in the circle of humankind, is likely to aggravate rather than overcome the causes of war. It is imperative on every level of human affairs to love those we reprove.

Compassion also overcomes estrangement. Even imperfect love has better prospects of bringing people together than does the most skillfully orchestrated exercise of moralistic judgmentalism. We will be compassionate to the extent that we acknowledge our solidarity with others in the creating of suspicion and contention. Augustine once observed that it is wise to love our enemies because so often we are our own worst enemy. That enemy within has to be reconciled to us in love, not vanquished with repression. The same is true about enemies without.

Compassion and reconciliation also make life different by giving the service of human need a higher claim than partisan loyalty. Is this not one of the truths made clear by the story of the good Samaritan? Both priest and Levite failed to help, not least we may suppose because they realized that the victim in the roadway belonged to a different social group. Furthermore, they may have feared that their ceremonial purity would be compromised by association with the victim. The Samaritan, already a member of an outcast group, would not have been inhibited from association with any victim.

There is much argument going on today as to whether church bodies should give contributions for the alleviation of human needs in groups that hold different or antagonistic points of view. Those who are disturbed by the distribution of such funds contend that the political and ideological complexion of groups has to be evaluated positively before they can be given even humanitarian assistance. Such a position is consistent with the premises of conflict, according to which partisanship is the most important consideration. But, if human need has a higher claim than political identification, then a different response seems appropriate. We should take the risk involved in meeting human need wherever it is found and trust that a better future will emerge from reconciliation and compassion than will come from hostility and polarization.

VI

From Indifference to Advocacy and Action

No thinking about the foundations of peacemaking can be adequate without a discussion of the ways and means by which it is possible to do those things that make for peace. The word "do" appears in the Bible almost four times as often as the word "believe," over ten times as frequently as the word "repent," and nearly five times as frequently as the word "understand." Acting and doing are essential parts of Christian discipleship. Faith must lead to action or, as the current "in word" states it, to praxis. "You are my friends," said Jesus to those who would be his followers, "if you do what I command you" (John 15:14).

INNER PEACE AND PUBLIC SERVICE

In thinking about the action side of peacemaking, we must begin with ourselves. Action for peace is integrally linked to qualities of our personal being. Our personal attitudes are as important as our structural involvements. Any sharp incongruity between our private behavior and our official roles will undercut the credibility of what we do. It is not likely that we will contribute much to the peace of the world if we are not at peace with ourselves and with those who are closest to us. In teaching the disciples about the nature of Christian living, Christ said to them, "If you are offering your gift at the altar, and there remember that your brother [read: associate!] has something against you, leave your gift there before the altar and go; first be reconciled to your [associate] and then come and offer your gift" (Matt. 5:23–24). Christ might also have said, "If you are engaged in some voluntary service or in some action for peace, and there remember . . ."

The peacemaker's own peace is important. Unless we know the love of God as a reconciling experience in our own lives, how can we believe that reconciliation is possible in the life of the world? If we believe that there are continuities and similarities between intimate human relationships and the relationships that ought to exist between larger groups, then we cannot escape the realization that the qualities of the self that make possible the most fruitful human relationships between close associates are necessary for creating fruitful relationships on a larger scale. The manipulation of social outcomes by itself will not do. The peacemaker must be a peaceful person.

In their *Handbook for World Peacemaker Groups*, authors Gordon Cosby and Bill Price set forth twin concepts of the Inward Journey and the Outward Journey. They suggest that to prepare for the Inward Journey a person make this resolve:

> I commit myself to search for an ever-deepening understanding and appropriation of Christ's gift of inner security and peace. I recognize that this entails a serious journey inward until the sources of fear and violence within me are touched and understood and in a beginning way transmuted. I understand there will be no outer peace until there is inner peace.

In preparing for the Outward Journey a person may make this resolution:

> I commit myself to search for ways of (1) encouraging our nation and all nations to eschew armaments and violence as a means for national and world security and (2) building a strong nation based on spiritual rather than military security. I recognize that this entails a serious outward journey implementing in the world's structures the peace imperative discovered in the inward search.[19]

We must not let presence at the altar be split apart from the experience of reconciliation. Most liturgies have in them a time when "the peace" is given and when members of the congregation may greet each other, saying, "Peace be with you." This action makes the altar, or whatever equivalent of standing exposed before God is vital in a particular tradition, a very real aspect of peacemaking. It is no accident that some of the greatest interest in peace has come from those who, like Thomas Merton, have been vocationally committed to the contemplative life. The things that we do (and that are done for us) in worship are crucial means of becoming prepared to make peace. In worship we focus attention on the justice, mercy, and empowering grace of God, and thus are helped to see that there are realities beyond naked power and worldly intrigues. In worship we stand in humble awareness of the inadequacies of our resolves and the inherent limitations of our abilities to do the things we must, and thus are helped to see that not everything can depend upon how we push it around. In worship our attention is focused upon all the other human beings that are objects of God's care, and thus we are prepared to be reconciled to them. In worship we are given the blessing that is offered to those who will accept it in humility and trust, and thus are helped to face life with equanimity.

When God is truly worshiped (in any of many moving and significant ways), persons are prepared to live in gratitude to God and in harmony with each other. The word "peace" (or, *shalom*) is said very often in worship, and if the word "Amen"—which has connotations of the proper ordering and resting of things—is understood as an affirmation of peace, the count goes way up. Moreover, as if to reinforce the reciprocity between the altar and peace, it is also the case that worship will be most meaningful to those who are engaged in an active search for peace. Hence, if the words at the altar have become mere formalisms (or the nonwords in private meditation are empty), go and get involved in some reconciling action and peacemaking and then come back and hear the words spoken in worship (or in the silent heart) with fresh and newly powerful meaning.

ROOM FOR DIVERSITY

There is no one single way to act for peace. Peacemaking can take many forms. Each of us stands in a different role in relation to the making of peace. It is our task to discover the uniqueness of our role and to carry it on with as much dedication and skill as we can marshal. The Baden Consultation on Christian Concern for Peace, which in 1970 brought together representatives of the World Council of Churches and the Pontifical Commission on Justice and Peace, said this about the ways and means of education for peace: "The methods of education for peace must be pluralistic, experimental, centered in learning through community action when possible and centered on persons always."[20] What is true about education for peace is true of every other form of service we render to establish well-being and goodwill among persons. There is no single way to do the things that make for peace.

Just as an ear cannot say to an eye, "The body has no

need of you," so a person who works for peace in one way cannot say to someone who works for peace in another way, "Your contribution is of no account." A monk and a student active in peace movements once had a conversation. The monk said: "Every morning at five o'clock I am praying for peace. What are you doing?" The student replied, "I am asleep recuperating from the hard study of issues in which I was engaged until three o'clock." Neither was entitled to judge the service rendered by the other as unacceptable or irrelevant.

Some people will find they can best work for peace by taking part in campaigns and demonstrations. Others will find that they can teach. Still others will find their best contribution to come from analytical thinking and writing. Each needs the others. Few can do all things well, and none has time to do everything completely. It is of the very nature of peace to permit different people to do different things toward its establishment, to stress different ways of making it real, to honor a variety of gifts in the service of a common objective.

In contrast, wars and preparations for wars demand far more conformity and uniformity. Military units do not function on the premise that voluntary cooperation between individually diverse parties brings about the swift completion of an appointed mission. Military training is premised on the subjugation of individual agenda to group procedures, on the insistence that all parties proceed even to think the same way. Conformity and loyalty are collapsed into an indistinguishable unity. Close-order drill and mass-produced uniforms, which are common features of modern warfare, may have been introduced relatively late in the history of armies, but their grip upon the military way of acting and thinking has been strong ever since. Only the appearance of guerrilla tactics in insurgency warfare has broken the correlation between the making of war and the pursuit of conformity in human relationships.

Nor does the conformity, or the pressure to conformity, affect only those who join military units in wartime. The conduct of a foreign policy that is based upon military strength is often marked by a pressure to think in a standardized way about how things are to be understood and how obligations are to be accepted. The enemy is to be feared (and perhaps even hated) by everyone; the defense effort is to be placed "beyond politics" and to be accorded the unconditional loyalty of everyone. Those who dare to question or resist the controlling ethos are branded "traitors," "enemies," or "infidels." Those who rely on the making of war for ordering human life are notoriously prone to believe that those who are not completely and unreservedly with us are against us. President Ronald Reagan, late in 1982, demonstrated the pervasiveness of such thinking when, in commenting on the advocates of a nuclear freeze, he said that they were being duped "by some who want the weakening of America."[21]

Almost all totalitarian regimes depend upon the trappings of military pageantry and procedures to cement their power over people. The same dynamic works in democracies during wartime conditions. A belief that the affairs of the globe can be kept in order only by the use, or threatened use, of force works at cross-purposes with a view that people can do things freely, and in many different ways, as they seek to wrestle with issues of justice, order, truth, and well-being. Peacemakers can believe that those who are not against us are for us. They can welcome differences and be open to the possibility that a viable social order can be served in many different ways, not least by those who are called to challenge the sanctity accorded official actions and to speak truth to power in the name of faith.

It has often been suggested that Christians seeking to be socially responsible should think as public officials have to think. Otherwise, what Christians say will lack credibility and cannot be translated into public policy. This may be true about thinking that limits a Christian's possibility to what can be done in military ways through the political channels of sovereign states alone.

But peacemaking can be a broader task. Peacemakers may have suggestions to offer public officials. They may also have suggestions to offer other Christians, both in their own country and in other lands. Peacemaking does not require the imprimatur of government to do its work. Just as many things in a free and pluralistic democracy are accomplished by groups that come together for the voluntary achievement of many objectives, so groups in the world whose identity transcends the official structures of the nation-states can be very important. One of the most exciting and widespread of such groups is the worldwide church, and some of the most exciting peacemaking is possible under its auspices. Members of the church can interchange information, compare ideas, cooperate on common projects across national boundaries, and argue vehemently among themselves without repudiating a common loyalty to Christ. Such diversity is the stuff of which peace is made.

STUDY AND ADVOCACY AS PEACEMAKING

One way of doing something for peace is to extend the range, the scope, and the depth of understanding about the issues and to share the deepened insights with others. The gathering and mastery of information is a form of empowerment. Those who "do their homework" frequently speak most persuasively. The power of information to change people's minds and to alter the dynamics of the political process varies from issue to issue and from country to country. Careful study may be most effective in open societies, and particularly so when undertaken with an official mandate. Such was the case in Israel in the work of the special commission appointed to study the Beirut massacres and to recommend follow-up actions. Similarly, the Cox Commission, which studied the actions of public officials at Watergate, was possibly more influential than might have been an unofficial group.

Not all official studies get implemented, to be sure, and unofficial studies can be effective. The prophets of Israel did not wait for kingly mandates to take a long hard look at Israel's behavior. Jonathan Schell, who spent a year in researching and writing his book *The Fate of the Earth,* [22] impacted the thinking of the American public about the dangers and possible consequences of an unlimited nuclear arms race. His book, which first appeared as three articles in a magazine,[23] may well have greatly affected the public's attitude toward the nuclear freeze.

One of the most interesting and important of recent efforts to influence public thinking has been the effort of the Roman Catholic bishops in America to draw up a pastoral letter on war and peace. To be sure, the Catholic bishops do have a public visibility that few other ecclesiastics can match, and they skillfully orchestrated a public discussion of the issues by releasing proposed versions of the letter as much as a year before they intended to set it forth in final form. Some of the attention received by this document arose from the fact that the normally conservative bishops were developing a position critical of an existing governmental policy. Moreover, while Protestant peace groups have long raised such issues on pacifist grounds, to have the Roman Catholic bishops do so on just war grounds was an unexpected turn of events. It is a mild understatement to suggest that the reaction of the Administration was one of deep concern, and it scurried to counter the effects of the letter, both by having conferences with the bishops to prod them to revise some of their language, and more broadly by mounting a major effort to discredit the position the bishops were advocating.

Any group in our society is free to counter the arguments and reasoning of the pastoral letter, and the quality of our political life can be enhanced to the extent that such freedom is exercised with skill and care. Debate is fostered by advocacy and counteradvocacy on substantive issues. It is precisely because such debate is impossible, or sadly curtailed in many countries, that we see ourselves uneasy about the spread of their influence. But it is utterly self-contradictory to argue that issues should never be raised about the policies of our Government because doing so might undercut its efforts to stand firm against countries that prohibit or curtail the free discussion of ideas.

We need a far better informed discussion of public issues than we already have. Perhaps the debate we most need is whether the American media sufficiently nourish such a debate. Some news programs attempt to do so, particularly those prepared for national consumption or for public broadcasting outlets. It is difficult to portray political events and to interpret what those events mean. They can be understood in many different ways, and reporting of the news does not always find it possible to canvass all possible meanings of the events upon which it reports. It requires a major investment of time to give both an adequate picture of what is happening and the range of perspective needed to discuss the implications of events. Perhaps we most need to suspect a readied diet of information that can be passively imbibed with little effort.

Some newspapers raise the same concerns as the broadcast media. Overly condensed, badly headlined, and slanted accounts do not suffice. Other newspapers contain extensive background materials about world events. Those who care about peace will read good newspapers as thoroughly as possible. A number of magazines and journals also portray the world scene with some depth and from a variety of perspectives. Too few homes have such magazines available to them on a regular basis.

Recent years have seen the development of a number of special centers or institutes devoted to the examination of policy issues. These are often called think tanks and they are something of a hybrid between an academic institution that professes a neutral objectivity in the treatment of issues and an avowedly political organization. They are often staffed by professor types or by ex-career public officials.

These centers have not managed to settle policy matters by impartially canvassing issues. In fact, some of them are driven by clearly evident, though not always acknowledged, ideologies taken from the particular perspectives of special groups. Some of them have become involved with the media, not so much to prompt the media to more careful examination of issues as to push a particular line. These think tanks, with some exceptions, have not brought about a deeper resolution of the policy issues that vex us. Suspicions between them are not unknown. It is all too easy to become "tainted" with a particular ideological bias by becoming associated with some of them or by participating in the programs that they sponsor. We must learn how to assess the output of such centers. We should be particularly on the alert when the output of any one of them sounds more like the work of a carping critic than like a lover's quarrel with the object of its scrutiny.

Just as the partisanship of politics sometimes makes statecraft difficult, but not impossible, so this introduction of partisanship into advocacy makes fairness difficult, but not unattainable. People know that in political campaigns differing points of view each try to state their own side as convincingly as possible. But they may uncritically accept a policy analysis of a think tank as an already balanced treatment of an issue. Perhaps some of these centers ought to combine in the joint sponsorship of a conference to explore issues in a broadly spectrumed, yet still confrontational, manner. In academic partisanship, as in politics itself, it is the possibility of mutual correction that makes advocacy safe.

The sponsorship of a policy study center will make quite a difference in its credibility. Those centers funded by a few large grants coming from sources having much the same point of view will not be so credible as those that are supported by more diverse constituencies. Those with governing boards that are self-selected for a given point of view will be less likely to treat issues fairly than those that have governing boards which are more diverse, the members of which are answerable (even in unofficial ways) to other groups. The more points of view from our society and the more societies from around the world that get heard in the deliberations of a think tank, the more dependable its analysis of situations is apt to be.

Churches that maintain ecumenical ties or have branches in many parts of the world constitute fine channels of international communication. The Roman Catholic Church is a multinational operation. Many Protestant denominations have also become internationalized by years of mission activity. They are invaluable sources of information about what is going on in other countries. Many denominations have more members in other countries, particularly south of the equator, than they do in their American constituencies. This is why gatherings of Christians quite often provide opportunities to see and to engage in dialogue with persons living in many places and seeing the world and its problems from many perspectives. Such gatherings, particularly if important issues are being contended and frankly discussed, are far more helpful in learning what is going on in the world than superficial tourism or even than studies (however well funded) that are done with reference only to the stance of one country. Experiencing confrontation and encountering differences of outlook constitute a better basis for making policy than relying upon standard impressions from one culture alone. People who do not sense where and why they differ cannot be reconciled. Only as we hear those who feel they have claims against us will we know why there are tensions in the world.

Not all such encounters are confrontational. Many times they will be surprisingly gratifying. We should make efforts to have exchanges with Christians from other places, particularly with those from places with which as a nation we are most in tension. It is often possible to arrange such events. For instance, in 1982 the peacemaking program of the United Presbyterian Church arranged to have Protopresbyter Vitaly Borovoy of the Russian Orthodox Church be a guest of certain American parishes. In June of that year he visited a Presbyterian church in Buffalo, New York. Reporting on the visit, a pastor of the church tells about several touching events that took place as members of the church ate, talked, and exchanged ideas with this Soviet church leader.

> During Sunday's worship a fourth-grader, David Schultz, presented Father Borovoy a banner created by the children in an earlier peace fair. The banner is bright blue with a collage of people holding hands. Its title reads "Brothers and Sisters in Christ." In receiving the gift for the children of his church, Father Borovoy embraced David, and with a voice filled with emotion spoke of his concern for the children in his country who could not attend worship. He concluded by saying, "Let us hope that this gift and message will be a sign of our common yet completely different good future in hope and love and in devotion and commitment to our common God."[24]

Perhaps weekend visits such as Father Borovoy made to Buffalo are merely inconsequential niceties on the periphery of the great raging power struggles that really count, but who knows for sure? Those suppers in an American parish may portend a saving future while nuclear arms are the mechanical dinosaurs of an outmoded era. The last supper of Christ didn't hold a candle to the power of Rome, but it now causes millions of candles to be lighted every day as the Eucharist is celebrated all over the world.

AN ACTION SIDE TO PEACEMAKING

Christians who are concerned about peacemaking will find themselves committed to different strategies for working toward peace. They may even argue about which strategies are most legitimate, which most productive. Only if we think of peacemaking as a kind of "warfare against war" will we insist that there is only one worthwhile or legitimate action to be taken on behalf of peace. There ought not to be a conscription of conscience in the cause of peace any more than there ought to be a conscription of conscience in time of war.[25]

With this in mind, let us describe some actions that can embody a peacemaking concern and mention some (by no means all) of the organizations that work in the different ways suggested by the kinds of things that can be done for peace.

One type of peace action alleviates some particular need or focuses on the amelioration of a particular kind of problem. For example, Amnesty International directs attention to the denial of human rights that occurs in every part of the world. It organizes letter-writing campaigns on behalf of those imprisoned for the sake of conscience and it makes periodic reports of high credibility on the status of human rights from country to country. Bread for the World is committed to the alleviation of hunger and uses the political system to encourage governmental programs toward this end. It organizes lobbying efforts to further these objectives. The American Friends Service Committee has a long and enviable record of relieving human need around the world and also a branch that holds up humanitarian concerns before the minds of public officials. The Interfaith Center on Corporate Responsibility monitors the policies of giant companies and on occasion challenges their policies by the use of proxy power. Many church groups have relief and rehabilitation agencies that work to alleviate human misery in a variety of ways. People can give their money or their talents to the work done by many of these organizations without having to embrace any particular theological or ideological ways of understanding war/peace issues.

Another way to take direct action on behalf of peace is through those organizations that are working to extend international order. Sometimes, as in the work of the United Nations Association, the concern to extend international order expresses itself as an effort to raise public consciousness about the importance of that organization for maintaining peace in the world. At other times the concern is to develop world order along more organic lines. The World Federalists Association favors a more organic kind of international cooperation than we have under the present system of national sovereignties. The Institute for World Order emphasizes the importance of security systems based upon cooperation between the nations. To work in these groups presupposes a commitment to a more particular judgment about how the world should be organized than to work in the groups that tackle specific projects, like relief or rehabilitation.

A third category of peace action is carried on by groups, often of an ecclesiastical nature, that call for a more intentional dedication—usually embodying a different lifestyle. The Church of the Saviour, a local parish in Washington, D.C., is a fine example of such a group. Its members are committed to certain disciplines as well as to certain doctrines. The Church of the Saviour created, and now stays actively interested in, the work of World Peacemakers, which consists of local units that are loosely associated under the common name but carry on their own activities. The World Peacemakers groups endorse a moratorium on the production, testing, and deployment of nuclear weapons. They see this as a first step toward disarmament and as part of an effort to bring about a redirecting of national priorities from military expenditures to programs that better serve human needs. A group with a Mennonite background, called Dunamis, is also interested in the relationship between life-style and peacemaking. The Fourth World Movement is made up of the very poor wherever they live, full-time volunteers who live with the poor, and those who support its work. It carefully documents the conditions of extreme poverty and encourages the poor to stand up for themselves. It is particularly concerned with families, children, and human rights. Like many of the other groups mentioned in this overview it has attained status as a nongovernmental organization (NGO) with the Economic and Social Council of the United Nations.

A fourth type of action, in some respects similar to the first, undertakes special projects to alleviate hunger and misery overseas. The American Friends Service Committee has done this for many years. A number of church groups, usually working through Heifer Project International, send food-producing animals to countries with hunger problems. International Voluntary Service, the Mond-Civitan Republic, Service Civil International, and short-term mission programs of several denominations also provide significant opportunities for service by those who wish to dedicate a part of their life to the advancement of peace by improving human well-being. Those who cannot go in person can support such work with money.

Those organizations that are primarily devoted to war resistance often contribute to peacemaking. They are usually composed of people holding pacifist convictions. Organizations like the Fellowship of Reconciliation, the War

Resisters League, the Peace Pledge Union, and the peace fellowships of several denominations often witness against the dangers of military power and the futility of seeking to resolve international disagreements by the use of force. These fellowships often support persons who refuse to participate in war, or in preparations for war, on the grounds of conscience.

The early 1980s has seen a proliferation of groups concerned with disarmament. Some work for general disarmament; others, for nuclear disarmament; still others, for a temporary freeze to buy time for negotiating reductions in the levels of armaments. Groups working for either nuclear or general disarmament include Mobilization for Survival, the Riverside Church Disarmament Program, and SANE: A Citizens' Organization for a Sane World. The World Peacemakers groups, which have already been mentioned, also concentrate heavily on the disarmament agenda.

In addition to working with the kinds of groups of which those cited are representative, we must be concerned with the political system. It is not difficult to decry the condition of the political process in America. Not enough people vote to make electoral decisions as representative as they ought to be. The presidency often suffers from repeated instances of public disillusionment. Congressional achievements are slow and difficult because of constituency fragmentation and the fact that the political parties are often as torn within themselves as between themselves. Moreover, the allocation of military expenditures is one of the most powerful means by which members of Congress serve their districts.

Many people were surprised by the referenda in 1982 that put the nuclear freeze question directly on the ballots of many electoral units. These provided, as elections have not always provided, a chance to use the voting booth as a direct expression of opinion on a peace issue. It nudged the political process in an unprecedented way and may well be a model for other similar efforts. Involvement in the political process can be an important way to make some difference in the things that make for peace.

People are bound to argue about the appropriateness of one or another strategy for making peace. A growing number of Christians are advocating a refusal to pay part of their taxes as a means of witnessing against national policies that increase world tension. Many other Christians, conveniently forgetting the Boston Tea Party as part of America's heritage, are indignantly opposed to that way of making a witness. Feelings are beginning to run high. It could be a time of testing for the premise that action for peace can take many forms.

Those who work for peace will do best if they keep open the process of exchanging ideas, if they respect the differing commitments of others, and if they give persons of many persuasions love and support. The freedom that counts the most is the freedom that enables any of us to risk something in a worthwhile cause and be accepted for doing so. Only those who know how to respect different ways of doing that will live together peacefully.

Epilogue

This book has taken issue with those who hold that interactions between large groups are amenable to control only by the use of force or by a credible threat to use force. It has argued that many of the same, or very similar, moral foundations upon which viable relationships between individuals and small groups must rest are necessary for making the larger relationships of human life more peaceful.

Nothing in this argument is intended to obscure the fact that violence is an ever-present reality on all levels of our experience. Two million American families are plagued by domestic violence. The battering of spouses and maltreatment of children is known at least once in three out of five households and affects many households on a repeated basis. Communities are afflicted by angry behavior of blood-chilling and even of blood-letting dimensions. In a nearby suburb three teenagers accosted another in a recent blizzard, roughing him up and leaving him unconscious in a snowdrift on a bitterly cold night. Muggings are endemic in many places and are possible anywhere. Hate mail is received by almost every public figure, and bitterness can be observed in a number of places where people interact with one another. Labor violence, which has significantly subsided in recent decades, is still known to occur in tense circumstances.

This violence knows no particular social or economic confines. It is not restricted to any part of the world nor to any political system. If tooth and claw characterize the animal world, clenched teeth and torture claws are all too characteristic of the human world. Instruments of pain and devastation devised by humans to force others to do their bidding approach levels of horror the animal world could never create. We have made enough military weaponry to destroy most of the centers of civilization in just a few minutes if the linchpin comes out of the global grenade. "The whole head is sick, and the whole heart faint," wrote Isaiah about ancient Jerusalem. "From the sole of the foot even to the head, there is no soundness in it, but bruises and sores and bleeding wounds; they are not pressed out, or bound up, or softened with oil" (Isa. 1:5b–6). We might be tempted to write much the same thing about our world, or many aspects of it.

A very common response to this specter of violence and hostility is to seek protection by mastering the control of counterviolence. Since the world is unstable, it is natural to seek security by possessing arms, or by the distribution of arms to those nations or groups which we think can possess them to our advantage. These responses to violence are understandable—the more so because they seem realistic. Unlike the people of Jeremiah's time, who cried " 'Peace, peace,' when there is no peace" (Jer. 8:11), we are apt to shout "Arms, arms, because there is no safety." A world of assassins, rebels, and fanatics seems to leave no alternative but to shine the brass and keep the neutrons functional—even if we have to do so, not by eliminating tax write-offs for business entertainment, but by cutting school lunches. When the world gets tough the tough get going. Hope for peace, but get ready for war.

The world is doing that today at the rate of a million dollars every minute.

But, says Paul in the letter to the church at Rome (faced as it was with similar contradictions between the realities of the world and the vision of faith), "do not be conformed to this world but be transformed by the renewal of your mind" (Rom. 12:2a). Learn God's will and the moral imperative of faith and thus overcome the calculating realism that turns self-concern into a cynical malignancy. This bold prescription needs to be taken very seriously, not least by those who profess to hold that the Bible is an important guide to faith and morals. This bold prescription puts a premium upon acquiring a new mind-set. The text of Paul is remarkably similar to an observation once made by President Anwar Sadat that "he who cannot change the very fabric of his thought will never be able to change reality."

In the passage from Romans, Paul suggests several dimensions to the change that can alone bring renewal. First, he says, "I bid every one among you not to think of yourself more highly than you ought to think, but to think with sober judgment" (Rom. 12:3a). At another place in the same chapter Paul suggests, "Do not be haughty, but associate with the lowly; never be conceited" (v. 16b).

Paul's admonitions to avoid moral arrogance can be applied to both personal and international relationships. Indeed, because we sense more immediately the serious consequences of arrogance in close encounters we tend to keep it controlled. But it gets out of bounds between the nations, which is why conflict arises. Nations do not make wars until they think of themselves more highly than they ought to think. They make war only when they think that their cause is so righteous that it is legitimate, not merely to die, but to kill for it. The most demonic group behavior is likely to arise from nations that regard themselves as almost angelic.

In 1981 a group of ninety-three nations, claiming to be nonaligned in the great ideological divide that characterizes the current international situation, issued a document declaring that the United States is the only threat to peace and prosperity in the contemporary world.[26] The document listed the standard grievances such as our downing of two aircraft over what Libya considers open ocean. This document is certainly a shocker, particularly to ears accustomed to hearing the Soviet Union characterized as the only threat to peace. Either simplistic view cloaks an arrogance. Subsequently these same nations have prepared another paper equally blaming the United States and the Soviet Union for threatening the peace.[27] Even this second statement may be too simple, but it clearly shows that many nations fear both major powers.

How, then, do we deal with such perceptions? First, by not thinking of ourselves so highly as to make it impossible to find out why so many nations could be led to make such statements. We need to sense—to understand—the feelings prompting those words, the dynamics of a world in which numerous nations want justice and find our posture and policies one of the obstacles to having it. We need to realize why nations want to be treated in terms of their authenticity and their own aspirations and not merely in terms of how subservient they are to the cold war conflict.

This brings us to Paul's second way of portraying the qualities of the renewed mind that alone can transform our response to the circumstances we confront. Paul speaks about coming to know our oneness with all humanity—a oneness that he speaks about in terms of the body of Christ, in which there are numerous members working harmoniously with each other. Perhaps this is why Paul urges us to "bless those who persecute us" and "not to repay evil for evil." We will not be able to know our oneness in Christ unless we find ways to sense our oneness with enemies as well as with friends.

Paul is talking about love. There is nothing about love that requires sentimentality. Love is the opposite of hatred and anger, not the opposite of just and tough demands. When love makes a tough demand, as it does frequently, it always arranges to stand-under, supporting those upon whom the demand is made—to reinforce, to encourage, and to aid the person or the group upon whom the obligation is laid.

We know that such under-standing is crucial in maintaining good dynamics within families. Good parents make demands, but they also understand. In contrast to angry parents who merely criticize and scold or sentimental parents who cease to expect anything, loving parents both require things of their children and support them in fulfilling the requirements. They also demand as much of themselves as they expect from others.

But what does it mean to be loving in larger structural relationships? Can we be loving between nations? Can we renew our minds so as to speak fairly and candidly, defending justice and human well-being, while encouraging both those who readily respond and those who don't, so that our relationship to them is founded, not on superiority, disdain, or anger, but on mutuality and trust? The answer to this question is only beginning to be explored. The call to put our minds to work at peace thinking is important and deserves our response, however feeble or difficult it may be at first. It is better to blow our minds with the urgency of the issues than to have homes and bodies blown to bits. We need to believe, with Paul, that our minds and hearts can be transformed, that we need not rush headlong toward destruction, and that times of urgency and danger are also opportunities for renewal. There is no greater opportunity in these times than to believe this with understanding.

Notes

1. Alan Geyer, *The Idea of Disarmament: Rethinking the Unthinkable* (Brethren Press and The Churches' Center for Theology and Public Policy, 1982), p. 191.

2. See Edward LeRoy Long, Jr., *War and Conscience in America* (Westminster Press, 1968), Chs. 4 and 5.

3. George F. Kennan, *The Nuclear Delusion: Soviet-American Relations in the Atomic Age* (Pantheon Books, 1982), p. 201.

4. Paul Ramsey, *The Just War: Force and Political Responsibility* (Charles Scribner's Sons, 1968), p. 494.

5. Richard L. Rubenstein, from an unpublished paper presented to a study group of the Council on Religion and International Affairs in 1971. Used by permission of the author.

6. John Rawls, *A Theory of Justice* (Harvard University Press, Belknap Press Book, 1971).

7. Robert Nozick, *Anarchy, State, and Utopia* (Basic Books, 1974).

8. John R. Donahue, "Biblical Perspective on Justice," in John C. Haughey, ed., *The Faith That Does Justice: Examining the Christian Sources for Social Change* (Paulist Press, 1977), p. 91.

9. Waldron Scott, *Bring Forth Justice* (Wm. B. Eerdmans Publishing Co., 1980).

10. Fyodor Dostoevsky, *The Grand Inquisitor*, tr. by Constance Garnett with reflections on the story by William Hubben (Association Press, A Haddam House Book, 1948), p. 21.

11. Ibid., pp. 18f.

12. Eduard Heimann, *Freedom and Order: Lessons from the War* (Charles Scribner's Sons, 1947), p. 6.

13. Geyer, *The Idea of Disarmament,* p. 194.

14. Quoted in Mark Sullivan, *Our Times: The United States, 1900–1925,* Vol. 1 (Charles Scribner's Sons, 1926), pp. 47–48.

15. Kennan, *The Nuclear Delusion,* p. 30.

16. This is the phrase used by President Ronald Reagan in an address before the National Association of Evangelicals, Orlando, Florida, March 8, 1983. See *The New York Times,* March 9, 1983, p. A18.

17. Henri J. M. Nouwen, *With Open Hands* (Ave Maria Press, 1972), p. 112.

18. Rollo May, *Power and Innocence: A Search for the Sources of Violence* (W. W. Norton & Co., 1972), p. 250.

19. Gordon Cosby and Bill Price, *Handbook for World Peacemaker Groups* (World Peacemakers, 2852 Ontario Road, N.W., Washington, D.C. 20009, n.d.), p. 2.

20. *Peace—The Desperate Imperative,* The Report of the Consultation on Christian Concern for Peace (Baden, Austria, April 3–9, 1970), p. 43. This is an official report to the World Council of Churches and to the Pontifical Commission on Justice and Peace.

21. This phrase was used by President Reagan in a speech before a convention of five veterans groups in Columbus, Ohio, October 4, 1982. See *The New York Times,* Oct. 5, 1982, p. A22.

22. Jonathan Schell, *The Fate of the Earth* (Alfred A. Knopf, 1982).

23. Jonathan Schell, "Reflections: The Fate of the Earth," *The New Yorker,* Vol. 57: No. 50 (Feb. 1, 1982), pp. 47–81; No. 51 (Feb. 8, 1982), pp. 45–61; No. 52 (Feb. 15, 1982), pp. 45–61.

24. William L. Hathaway, in "Parish Peacemaking," *Monday Morning: A Magazine for Presbyterian Ministers,* Vol. 48, No. 3 (Feb. 7, 1983), p. 9.

25. For a discussion of this, see Long, *War and Conscience in America,* especially Ch. 5.

26. *The New York Times,* Oct. 5, 1981, p. A4.

27. *The New York Times,* Feb. 6, 1983, pp. 1 and 15.